CONTENTS

CONTENTS

PREFACE

There are many qualities we think about when deciding to bring a pet into our lives. Words like *loyal, smart, courageous, protective, tenacious,* and *playful,* probably top the list. Not surprisingly, they are also the very qualities that make the Parson Russell Terrier, also known as the Jack Russell Terrier, one of the most fascinating breeds in the dog world. The breed gained American Kennel Club recognition in 2001 as the Jack Russell Terrier. Then in 2003, the name was changed to the Parson Russell Terrier to conform to the name change adopted by the Kennel Club of Great Britain (see history of the breed, page 1). For the purposes of this book, the name Parson Russell Terrier will be used to comply with the AKC.

Regardless of whether you know him as a *Parson* or a *Jack,* you'll surely agree that not only is this little dog's "personality" far too big for his small size, but it's also one of his most engaging features. The Russell is a comedian and prankster extraordinaire who will bring an abundance of laughter into your home. Even when he's at his mischievous best, it's hard to stifle a smile. Maybe it's the special way he looks at you with that impish twinkle in his eyes, or that devilish charm that will not quit. No matter, having a Russell in your life is an experience that will change you both forever.

Originally bred as a working terrier, the Russell's ancestors had only one purpose: to serve their masters. If that meant digging tunnels deep into the dark earth to corner prey, or getting dirty in the subterranean levels of rodent-ridden castles to expunge vermin, then so be it. Standing little more than a foot and a half high, he had the heart of a bear, the courage of a lion, and the smarts to outfox the fox! The Russell was never intended to be a house pet, but his ability and delight in working closely beside his master eventually made him the perfect companion dog. Eighteenth-century sportsmen, chief among them Parson John Russell, from whom the Russell takes his name, prized their terriers as hunters and as pets. In fact, Parson Russell and his wife kept several favorite terriers in their home.

Over the centuries, the Russell has evolved from a primarily working terrier to a full-time house pet. With the exception of specialty clubs and competitions designed to preserve the breed's heritage, today's Russell has adapted to a different type of service—that of being the best companion a human owner can imagine.

Although this dog is not suited to everyone, he gives back one-hundred-fold to the owner willing to put in the time and effort to forge the strong bond of friendship and respect this breed demands. He would be the first to admit that he's a high-maintenance kind of dog. He demands a lot of your time and he's not above trying your patience, just to see if you've got the right stuff. If you pass muster, he'll be your lifelong best friend and your most loyal companion.

The purpose of this book is to celebrate this unique and special breed and most important, to reveal its true nature. Whether the Russell is the right breed for you or not, it is hoped that this book will give you a new appreciation and respect for this dynamic and devoted terrier who is happiest when he is by your side.

Chapter One

All About Parson Russell Terriers

He stands there at attention, a good two to three feet below your waist, totally undaunted by his small stature, totally focused, alert, and expectant as he gazes up at you with those amazingly intelligent, yet soulful, brown eyes. He may as well be talking to you:

Okay, Mom, what's next?

You answer him, just like you would any human being who posed the same question.

Let's go to the store, Jack.

He'll think a moment, tilt his head in acknowledgment, and away you'll both go to the next task.

Sound bizarre? Or maybe a just little off-the-wall? To some, perhaps, but certainly not to anyone who has ever shared their life with a Parson Russell Terrier. To them, it's just another day as usual with the best companion a human could ask for. The bond you've forged together didn't happen overnight. It took time, patience, and a growing sense of mutual respect. In fact, your journey together continues to be a learning experience, and that's what makes it so interesting and challenging. You continue to discover new things about each other every day, almost like an old married couple. It's a good feeling. It's a relationship that has become comfortable but never dull, secure but never without its exasperating moments, and you can't imagine life without it.

A Brief History

But who is this adorable, pint-sized dynamo, really? In truth, the answer is as intriguing as the dog himself, and it is equally incapable of being reduced to a solitary, straightforward explanation. The history of the Parson Russell Terrier, also known as the Jack Russell Terrier, is derived from both fact and legend. Where the one ends and the other begins remains, to this day, a subject of hot debate in many a fanciers' circle.

Let's begin with the facts. The single most important one is that terrier-type dogs have been in existence as far back as at least the sixth century in

1

Europe and probably even earlier throughout the British Isles. Noblemen gifted other nobles and even kings with terriers, which were much appreciated because castles, manor houses, and the like had dank, subterranean levels overrun with rats and other vermin. The singular function of the early terrier was to control the pest population. He was, if you will, the ancient version of today's Orkin Man! To do his work properly, the terrier had to have certain physical characteristics: He had to be small and agile enough to go underground, and hardy and courageous enough to flush out or, in the case of rodents, kill his prey.

Breed Truths

The name *terrier* comes from the Latin word *terra*, which means "earth." Because of his unique ability to *go to ground*, the terrier was also called an "earthdog." A terrier goes to ground when he follows quarry into a tunnel or a hold, sometimes many feet below ground, and traps it there while barking furiously to alert the hunter of its location. Terriers have been known to dig so deeply into the earth to corner prey that they have had to be dug out with heavy machinery.

The Russell, as we have come to know him, originated in Great Britain. From early drawings and illustrations (circa eighteenth century), it's clear that there was no standardization among terriers except that they mostly resembled rough-coated mongrels with undocked tails. Moreover, because travel from place to place was difficult, it was fairly commonplace to find a uniform strain of terrier indigenous to a specific region or locality. These early terriers or earthdogs lived hard, Spartan lives, and because of their working function, not much attention was paid to their looks. In fact, the white-bodied terriers we know today were rarely seen before the mid-eighteenth century in Great Britain because hunters associated the white color with congenital weakness.

By the middle of the eighteenth century, however, that thinking had begun to change as terriers were introduced into two increasingly popular and grisly "poor man's" sports: badger baiting and rat killing. Both were timed events that drew crowds akin to a modern-day local sports event.

In badger baiting, terriers were put into a hole, and the one who pulled the badger out the most times before the bell rang was declared the winner. In rat killing, a large number of rats were contained in a small arena-like enclosure. Terriers were then released into the arena and the massacre began. The dog who killed the most rats within the specified time won the day. These contests required a dog that possessed not only great strength and courage, but also superior speed and toughness. This led to crossbreeding the regional terriers with other breeds, notably the English Bull Terrier and the Pit Bulldog. The result was the strain of mostly white-bodied terriers from which the present-day Russell gets his color.

The bulldog of this era was a veritable terror, bred to bait and hold a bull by the nostrils while crowds cheered. His grip and his courage became

legendary. The only thing he lacked was the agility needed to be the star performer at badger-baiting and rat-killing contests. Thus, he was crossed with the terrier to create what was deemed the ideal dog for this new sports craze: a fast-moving, agile terrier with the grit of a bulldog.

In the nineteenth century, foxhunting, formerly the sport of kings, became the sport of choice among the English country set. Hounds ran ahead of mounted riders to snare the fox. But terriers were used to do the "dirty" work—that is, go to ground and flush out the fox from his hiding place so the hounds could give chase and the hunt could continue, ensuring a happy day for all, except the poor fox.

Despite the indispensable service they performed, terriers were fairly low on the totem pole. Unlike hounds, for which breeding registries were meticulously kept, registering terriers was not considered important since all that mattered was that the terrier was physically able to perform his rigorous task. As a result, terriers were crossed indiscriminately with other breeds to produce a dog that would fulfill the expectations of the master who kept them. A sportsman who wanted a terrier that was more aggressive with prey introduced bulldog into his breeding. Another who wanted a terrier with a more highly developed sense of smell introduced beagle into his stock. If more speed was desired, greyhound was used. Thus, at the time of Parson John Russell, a terrier was a *type* of dog rather than a specific breed.

The Legend of the Parson and Trump

Any attempt to appreciate or piece together the Russell's origins must now turn to a consideration of his namesake, Parson John Russell himself. Like his canine counterpart, aspects of the parson's life will always remain a

Fun Facts

John Russell definitely loved dogs more than his studies. In fact, during his student days, he was almost expelled from Oxford for keeping a small pack of foxhounds with a neighboring blacksmith. Before that, he nearly got his walking papers from The Tiverton School for a similar offense!

puzzle, if not a complete mystery. The extent of his influence in the actual development of the dog that would later bear his name remains questionable.

We do know that John Russell was born in Devon, England, on December 12, 1795. By that time, the predominantly white terrier was already on the scene. Like his father, John Russell chose the life of a clergyman. But far from the conventional image of a quiet, retiring man of the cloth, Parson Jack was a flamboyant, rollicking sportsman, who excelled at boxing and was not above skipping a Sunday sermon in favor of a chance to give chase with his hounds and terriers. According to D. Brian Plummer, author of *The Complete Jack Russell Terrier*, Russell was "an almost obsessional hunter [whose] predatory menagerie of ferrets, terriers and hounds were his lifelong pets and companions." Although Russell and his wife, Penelope, also a hunt enthusiast, kept hounds, they both seemed to prefer terriers.

According to the legend, circa 1819, around Oxfordshire, Russell, then a divinity student at Oxford, set his eyes on a rough-coated white terrier-type bitch with dark tan patches over the eyes and ears and a similar patch on the base of the tail. *Trump* was riding in the back of a milkman's cart. It must have been love at first sight, because Parson Jack, whose passion for working dogs was itself legendary, struck a deal with the milkman then and there and purchased the dog. According to accounts of the time, Russell felt that Trump's whole aspect personified the traits he most coveted in a hunting dog: courage, endurance, and hardiness.

It is said that Trump became the foundation bitch for the parson's breeding kennel. Russell seemed to have favored a compact, rough-coated, energetic white terrier with narrow shoulders and straight legs, standing 14 inches at the shoulder and weighing 14–16 pounds. Although he supposedly kept smooth-coated fox terriers as well, it was Russell's apparent fondness for the rough-coated variety that contributed to the popularity of the Wire-Fox Terrier, which remains one of the most popular breeds in England.

By the mid-nineteenth century, Parson Jack was well known as one of the West Country's leading breeders of fox terriers. However, there is also evidence that the parson was financially strapped from time to time, and thus made a living selling off his dogs and then buying more, as his fortunes dictated. For this reason, it is highly unlikely that he actually developed the strain of terriers that would later bear his name. Nonetheless, he probably purchased terriers that most conformed to his ideal and bred them to similar dogs he already owned. Indeed, Russell's own popularity contributed to the popularity of his dogs. Over time they became referred to as "Jack Russell" terriers to distinguish them from the other types of fox terriers.

John Russell reportedly despised terrier strains bred to be so aggressive that they would characteristically maim or kill the fox. Not only did Russell believe it was a very unsportsmanlike quality, but he also thought it destroyed the spirit of the chase. In Russell's opinion the perfect terrier was a courageous, agile, robust little dog whose job was to bay and flush the fox out of its hole. He thoroughly disapproved of the increasingly common practice among his fellow terrier men of using bulldogs in their breeding programs to keep the terrier rough and hard. The other cross added to this mixture was beagle, which gave the terrier a keener sense of smell and more voice. It is generally agreed that the present-day Russell, and indeed the present-day fox terrier, evolved indirectly from this mixture.

Breed Truths

As late as the 1930s, a British terrier man named Geoffrey Sparrow advocated crossbreeding with the bull terrier every ten generations to maintain courage and adequate jaw size in working terriers. This was not in keeping with the terrier favored by Parson Russell, who believed the dog was and should remain a baying terrier whose function was to bolt the quarry from its hole, not kill it.

In 1873, Parson Russell became one of the founding members of England's Kennel Club, and in 1874, he judged fox terriers in the club's first sanctioned dog show. It was to be his first and last time in the show ring. He never exhibited his own dogs, nor did he ever judge another show. According to the scuttlebutt of the day, Parson Jack thought that his dogs were superior to those he saw in the ring, as his comment seems to suggest: "True terriers they were, but differing from the present day show dogs as the wild eglantine differs from the garden rose." Russell and other dedicated terrier men banded together and maintained a strain of fox terriers bred strictly for working, not showing.

John Russell died in 1883. The four dogs he had left—Rags, Sly, Fuss, and Tinker—were given away. After his death, all predominatly white working terriers with similar markings were associated with Parson Russell, and the name "Jack Russell Terrier" was born. As a result, all types of working and hunting terriers were dubbed "Jack Russell's," even though they bore little to no resemblance to the terriers kept and bred by Parson Russell. Since

Russell never registered his own dogs or kept a written pedigree as far as we know, and also sold them indiscriminately, anyone could have claimed to have one of his dogs. Although there is no direct genetic link between Parson Russell's dogs and today's Russell, Russell's influence on type and size is undeniable.

In the years after Russell's death, the growing agricultural industry in the south of England practically made mounted foxhunting a thing of the past. Hunting devotees who had neither the land nor the money to keep up the sport came up with an alternative and began using terriers for fox and badger digging. All they had to do was release the dog down a hole. It would then burrow down and kill whatever it found. This variation of the sport required a different type of terrier—one that was aggressive, with shorter legs, a longer body, and a wider jaw span than the type favored by John Russell and his group of terrier men.

The Russell Evolution in England

With the advent of Kennel Club, a fox terrier craze began in England. In 1904, Arthur Heinemann, a younger contemporary of Parson Russell, drafted the first standard for the breed. It called for a 14-inch terrier, which reflected the original type favored by John Russell. Then in 1914, Heinemann founded The Parson Jack Russell Club, formerly called The Somerset Badger Digging Club. The name change is significant because the original purpose of the

club was to dig for badger and chase otters. These activities did not require as narrow a chest in the terrier as did chasing fox, indicating that Heinemann's type of terrier had already evolved from the strain bred by Parson Russell. Furthermore, Heinemann became a well-known dog dealer who sold his dogs throughout the United Kingdom and overseas. That Heinemann changed the name of his club was probably to identify his dogs with the most popular name in the terrier world, namely Jack Russell, rather than those known as merely Kennel Club Fox Terriers, and thereby command a better price.

Fun Facts

If you're visiting England, stop by Sandringham Castle in Norfolk, where a painting of Trump still hangs in the Harness Room. Or, in Barnstaple, you can stop in for a pint at The Jack Russell Inn, identifiable by a picture of Trump hanging outside!

By the turn of the century, the new name for these working terrier dogs had pretty much stuck, as evidenced in Robert Leighton's book *Dogs and All About Them* (1910), where he called them Jack Russell Terriers, not Parson Russell Terriers. The latter name change would come much later.

The Russell Today

Arthur Heinemann died in 1930, but his partner, Annie Rawls Harris, continued selling Jack Russells and kept the Parson Russell Terrier Club going until just before World War II. Then in 1974, The Jack Russell Club of Great Britain was founded "to promote and preserve the working terrier known as the Jack Russell" by Mrs. Romayne Moore, who had earlier founded the Midland Working Terrier Club. Mrs. Moore was instrumental in setting a standard that allowed any white, working terrier that conformed to a rough description of the Jack Russell Terrier to be registered. There was also an "advanced" register for dogs of purportedly higher quality. These dogs had to be at least 18 months old, and were reviewed by special inspectors. They also had to conform to a stricter standard regarding height, weight, and general structure. The point of the advanced register was to provide a standard of excellence that would encourage more desirable breedings. However, although the intentions of the club were good, in practice a strict standard was not achieved until much later.

The years between the Heinemann strain of terriers and the Moore renaissance are called the *lean years*. By the 1970s the height standard of 10–15 inches was wide enough to allow the inclusion of dogs that clearly distorted the original concept of breed function. It was during this time that the Russell first came to the United States. Many dogs were brought *across the pond* by people who had lived in England or by those who were visiting and brought a dog home with them. In 1976, the Jack Russell Terrier Club of America (JRTCA) was founded.

As the Jack Russell became increasingly popular in Great Britain, there was more pressure to pull it into the ranks of the Kennel Club and write a standard for the breed. But clearly there was a split of opinion between those who were adamantly opposed and those who favored Kennel Club recognition. As Jean and Frank Jackson wrote in their book, *Parson Jack Russell Terriers*, the Kennel Club advocates believed that "official recognition provides a framework of authority, access to reliable services, a means to national and international influence, and opportunity to become involved as equals with other recognized breeds, which can only be of benefit."

In 1990, those in favor of recognition got their wish. A standard was drawn up, calling for a dog standing 12–15 inches at the withers (shoulder). The dog was originally admitted as The Parson Jack Russell. In 1999, the UK Kennel Club changed the name to The Parson Russell Terrier. Then in 2005, the standard was revised again to include dogs ranging from 10 to 15 inches at the withers.

Meanwhile, in the United States— two clubs: The Jack Russell Terrier Club of America (JRTCA) and the Parson Russell Terrier Association of America (PRTAA)—split off based on their theories of how to preserve the original working terrier breed, which essentially revolved around the issue of AKC recognition. The JRTCA was opposed; the PRTAA was in favor. Nonetheless, in 2000, the dog was admitted to the ranks of the American Kennel Club as the Jack Russell Terrier. Then, in 2003, the AKC changed the name to the Parson Russell Terrier, as an accommodation to the PRTAA, which sought to be both consistent with the breed name in England and to distinguish the longer-legged AKC-registered dogs from the shorter-legged Jack Russell Terriers.

Breed Truths

Spanning is one of the most important physical measurements of the breed. The reason is that in order for the dog to fulfill its breed imperative, the size of the chest needs to be small enough to squeeze into an average-sized foxhole. To span your dog, place your hands (which should be "average sized") around his chest right behind his elbows. If you can touch your fingers together, your boy's chest passes muster. Both the PRTAA and the JRTCA require this procedure. However, whereas the JRTCA uses spanning only as a guide, the PRTAA and the AKC consider it extremely important to the dog's function.

The PRTAA

The Parson Russell Terrier Association of America (PRTAA), formerly the Jack Russell Terrier Breeder's Association (JRTBA) and later the Jack Russell Terrier Association of America (JRTAA), is an organization of Parson Russell Terrier breeders and owners dedicated to the promotion, breeding, working, and continuance of the traditional purebred Parson Russell Terrier that was bred and worked by Parson John Russell. The club was established in 1985

in response to growing concerns that the breed was being misrepresented as a short-legged dog. It supports the same balanced terrier supposedly favored by Parson Russell: one with a chest spannable by moderate-sized hands, straight legs with a good bend of stifle, predominantly white with head, tail, and occasional body markings, and an alert and ready temperament. The ideal height of a mature dog is 14 inches at the withers, and bitch, 13 inches at the withers.

From 1987 to 1997, some dedicated JRTAA members worked tirelessly to gain AKC recognition for the breed. This finally happened on November 1, 1997. In January 1998, the breed became eligible for all AKC events, including conformation participation in the Miscellaneous Class at all-breed AKC shows. The breed was admitted into the AKC Terrier Group on April 1, 2000, as The Jack Russell Terrier. The name of the breed was subsequently changed to the Parson Russell Terrier on April 1, 2003. The reason for this change was twofold: first, to distinguish the AKC "Parson" from the "Jack," a short-legged terrier longer in body than in height; and second to be consistent with the breed name in England, Europe, and Australia. For this reason, the club also changed its name to the Parson Russell Terrier Association of America. The PRTAA is the AKC Parent Club for the breed as well as the parent club for the breed in the United States. Its responsibility is to preserve the AKC breed standard. The standard for the breed was last revised on September 29, 2004.

The JRTCA

The Jack Russell Club of America maintains a registry for the Jack Russell Terrier in the United States. The JRTCA is the largest Jack Russell Terrier club and registry in the world. The club was founded to protect and preserve the unique characteristics and working heritage of the dog. The club is, and always has been, emphatically opposed to recognition of the Jack Russell Terrier by any kennel club or all-breed registry. The JRTCA believes that recognition will deal the death blow to the strain of sound, intelligent working terrier that has been preserved by dedicated fanciers for more than 100 years.

The JRTCA maintains a breed registry designed to preserve the Jack Russell Terrier as a healthy working breed, free from genetic faults and characteristics that would be detrimental to the breed. Whereas other registries will register entire litters at birth, the JRTCA does not. Instead, each application for registration is judged on the individual dog's merits, not on those of its parents.

The AKC versus the JRTCA

Although the Parson Russell Terrier and the Jack Russell Terrier are very similar, some would even say the same dog, the AKC and the JRTCA each have a separate standard. (The AKC sets the official standard for all breeds recognized in the United States; for the purposes of this book, its standard is the one used when referencing the Russell. However, because both clubs have as their mission the preservation of the breed, both standards are presented.)

Fun Facts

Calling all art aficionados. If you thought the Russell was just the subject of paintings, guess again. Brooklyn-born *Tillie*, who was featured in a CBS news special (April 15, 2007), has put her paws to more creative pursuits by painting "abstracts" that her owner, Bowman Hastie, claims go for up to $2,200 a pop! Tillie has had more than 17 solo exhibits in such art capitals of the world as Milan, Amsterdam, and Brussels. Thus far, Tillie has sold more than 100 original paintings. Creativity runs in the family, too. One of Tillie's sons seems to be set on a singing career!

BREED STANDARD
AKC vs. JRTCA

Standard	AKC
Characteristics/ Temperament	Bold and friendly. Athletic and clever. At work he is a game hunter, tenacious, courageous, and single minded. At home he is playful, exuberant and overwhelmingly affectionate. He is an independent and energetic terrier and requires his due portion of attention. He should not be quarrelsome. Shyness should not be confused with submissiveness. Submissiveness is not a fault. Sparring is not acceptable.
General Appearance	A natural appearance: harsh weatherproof coat with a compact construction and clean silhouette. The coat is broken or smooth. He has a small, flexible chest to enable him to pursue his quarry underground and sufficient length of leg to follow the hounds. The ideal height of a mature dog is 14" at the highest point of the shoulder blade; bitches, 13". Terriers whose heights measure slightly larger or smaller than the ideal are not to be penalized in the show ring, provided other points of their conformation, especially balance, are consistent with the working aspects of the standard.
Head	Strong and in good proportion to the rest of the body so the appearance of balance is maintained. Expression: keen, direct, full of life and intelligence. Skull: flat with muzzle and back skull in parallel planes. Fairly broad between the ears, narrowing slightly to the eyes. The stop is well defined but not prominent. Muzzle: Length from nose to stop is slightly shorter than the distance from stop to occiput. Strong and rectangular, measuring in width approximately $\frac{2}{3}$ that of the back skull between the ears. Jaws: Upper and lower are of fair and punishing strength.
Eyes	Almond shaped, dark in color, moderate in size, not protruding. Dark rims are desirable, however where the coat surrounding the eye is white, the eye rim may be pink.
Ears	Small "V" shaped drop ears of moderate thickness carried forward close to the head as to cover the orifice and pointing toward the eye. Fold is level with the top of the skull or slightly above. When alert, ear tips do not extend below the corner of the eye.

JRTCA

The terrier must present a lively, active, and alert appearance. He should impress with his fearless and happy disposition. It should be remembered that the Jack Russell is a working terrier and should retain these instincts. Nervousness, cowardice, or over-aggressiveness should be discouraged and he should always appear confident.

A sturdy, tough terrier, very much on his toes all the time, measuring between 10" and 15" at the withers. The body length must be in proportion to the height, and he should present a compact, balanced image, always being in solid, hard condition.

Should be well balanced and in proportion to the body. The skull should be flat, of moderate width at the ears, narrowing to the eyes. There should be a defined stop but not overpronounced. The length of the muzzle from the nose to the stop should be slightly shorter than the distance from the stop to the occiput. The nose should be black. The jaws should be powerful and well boned with strongly muscled cheeks.

Should be almond shaped, dark in color and full of life and intelligence.

Small "V" shaped drop ears carried forward close to the head and of moderate thickness.

Standard	AKC
Mouth	Teeth are large with complete dentition in a perfect scissor bite, i.e., upper teeth closely overlapping the lower teeth and teeth set square to the jaws.
Neck	Clean and muscular, moderately arched, of fair length, gradually widening so as to blend well into the shoulders.
Forequarters	Shoulders: Long and sloping, well laid back, cleanly cut at the withers. Point of shoulder sits in a plane behind the point of the prosternum. The shoulder blade and upper arm are of approximately the same length; forelegs are placed well under the dog. Elbows hang perpendicular to the body, working free of the sides. Legs are strong and straight with good bone. Joints turn neither in nor out. Pasterns firm and nearly straight.
Hindquarters	Strong and muscular, smoothly molded, with good angulation and bend of stifle. Hocks near the ground, parallel, and driving in action. Feet as in front.
Body	In overall length to height proportion, the dog appears approximately square and balanced. The back is neither short nor long. The back gives no appearance of slackness but is laterally flexible, so that he may turn around in an earth. Tuck-up is moderate. Chest: narrow and of moderate depth, giving an athletic rather than heavily-chested appearance; must be flexible and compressible. The ribs are fairly well sprung, oval rather than round, not extending past the level of the elbow.
Feet	Round, cat-like, very compact, the pads thick and tough, the toes moderately arched pointing forward, turned neither in nor out.
Tail	Docked so the tip is approximately level to the skull. Set on not too high, but so that a level topline, with a very slight arch over the loin, is maintained. Carried gaily when in motion, but when baiting or at rest may be held level but not below the horizontal.
Coat	Smooth and broken: whether smooth or broken, a double coat of good sheen, naturally harsh, close and dense, straight with no suggestion of kink. There is a clear outline with only a hint of eyebrows and beard if natural to the coat. No sculptured furnishings. The terrier is shown in his natural appearance not excessively groomed. Sculpturing is to be severely penalized.

JRCTA

Strong teeth with the top slightly overlapping the lower. Scissor bite is preferred; level bites are acceptable.

Clean and muscular, of good length, gradually widening at the shoulders.

The shoulders should be sloping and well laid back, fine at points and clearly cut at the withers. Forelegs should be strong and straight boned with joints in correct alignment. Elbows hanging perpendicular to the body and working free of the sides.

Should be strong and muscular, well put together with good angulation and bend of stifle, giving plenty of drive and propulsion. Looking from behind, the hocks must be straight.

The chest should be shallow, narrow and the front legs not too widely apart, giving an athletic, rather than heavily chested appearance. As a guide only, the chest should be small enough to be easily spanned behind the shoulders, by average-sized hands, when the terrier is in a fit, working condition. The back should be strong, straight and, in comparison to the height of the terrier, give a balanced image. The loin should be slightly arched.

Round, hard padded, wide, of cat-like appearance, neither turning in nor out.

Should be set rather high, carried gaily and in proportion to body length, usually about four inches long, providing a good hand-hold.

Smooth, without being so sparse as not to provide a certain amount of protection from the elements and undergrowth. Rough or broken coated, without being woolly.

Standard	AKC
Color	White, white with black or tan markings, or a combination of these, tri-color. Colors are clear. As long as the terrier is predominantly white, moderate body markings are not to be faulted. Grizzle is acceptable and should not be confused with brindle.
Gait	Movement or action is the crucial test of conformation. A tireless ground covering trot displaying good reach in front with the hindquarters providing plenty of drive. Pasterns break lightly on forward motion with no hint of hackney-like action or goose-stepping. The action is straight in front and rear.
Disqualification	Height under 12" or over 15". Prick ears, liver nose. Overshot, undershot or wry mouth. Brindle markings. Overt aggression toward another dog.
Faults	Shyness, hare feet, soft, silky, woolly, or curly topcoat, lacking undercoat, excessive grooming and sculpturing.

The Russell in Art

White-bodied fox-working terriers have appeared in art throughout the centuries, but were most prominently featured in paintings by British artist Sawrey Gilpin in the eighteenth century. Gilpin specialized in animal paintings, particularly of dogs and horses. His 1790 painting of *Pitch,* a white fox-working terrier with a spot above the tail and split-head markings, shows beyond a doubt that the present-day Russell can claim him as a relative.

The truth is the Russell has had a love affair with the public almost since he first appeared on the scene. Recall, if you will, the old RCA ad featuring a cute white terrier-type dog peering into an old-fashioned gramophone. The subject of the original nineteenth-century painting titled *His Master's Voice* was a sprightly dog named *Nipper*, born in 1884 in Bristol, England. He was said to be a mix of terrier and Pit Bull Terrier, which was one of the combinations that is thought to have figured into the evolution of the present day Russell. In other circles, Nipper was simply called a Jack Russell Terrier. Nipper was owned by painter Francis Barraud. Nipper got his name because he had the annoying habit of nipping visitors in the back of their legs, much to the amusement of his owner.

JRCTA

White should predominate (i.e., must be more than 51% white) with tan, black, or brown markings. Brindle markings are unacceptable.

Movement should be free, lively, well coordinated with straight action in front and behind.

Shyness, disinterest, overly aggressive, defects in bite, weak jaws, fleshy ears, down at the shoulder, barrel ribs, out at elbow, narrow hips, straight stifles, weak feet, sluggish or unsound movement, dishing, plaiting, toeing, silky or woolly coats, too much color (less than 51% white), shrill or weak voice, lack of muscle or skin tone, lack of stamina or lung reserve, evidence of foreign blood.

Three years after Nipper's death in 1898, Barraud painted another picture of the dog listening to a wind-up phonograph. A modified form of that painting became the trademark for the telecommunications giant RCA Victor.

Later on, a Nipper-clone appeared in TV commercials with his "son," a Jack Russell puppy named *Chipper*, who was added to the RCA family in 1991. To this day, real Russell's play the roles of both Nipper and Chipper, although Chipper has to be replaced more often since his character is a puppy! A four-ton replica of Nipper can be seen on the roof of the old RTA (former RCA distributor) building on Broadway in Albany, New York.

The Russell in Entertainment

The Story of Eddie

What TV fan hasn't tuned into the multi-award-winning sitcom *Frasier* to see Frasier's better half, the infamous *Eddie*? As any viewer will tell you, Eddie, whose off-camera name was *Moose*, could do everything but talk. In fact, many will swear that his priceless expression drew as many, and sometimes more, laughs than the scripted material. However, it was a penchant for chasing cats that led this troubled terrier to become one of TV's most famous pooches.

Originally owned by a Florida family, Moose was a typical Russell: He chewed everything in sight, barked incessantly, dug up the backyard, and refused to be housetrained. His family finally had enough and gave him to the manager of Birds and Animals Unlimited, a company that trained animals for TV and motion pictures. Moose was sent to Hollywood and put in the care of Mathilde de Cagny, a Los Angeles-based trainer working for the show-biz-animal company.

When Mathilde first met Moose, she realized immediately that the dog's bad behavior stemmed from boredom: He was a working dog with no work to do! As soon as she began to work with the hapless canine, his personality changed dramatically for the better. Why? He finally had a purpose in life. After six months of training, Moose auditioned for the role of Eddie, beating out dozens of seasoned canine actors.

Although *Frasier* won countless Emmy awards, Eddie was the only "actor" never nominated, a fact Moose lamented in his now famous autobiography, *My Life as a Dog*: "I don't care. I'm sick of the whole damn mess. I'm just going to keep doing good work and be satisfied with the knowledge that I'm loved by millions of adoring fans around the world. But if I ever have to play a depressed dog again, I won't have to act."

However, in his 1994 Emmy acceptance speech, actor Kelsey Grammer paid tribute to his canine sidekick, as he held up the award and said, "Most importantly, Moose, this is for you."

As Moose got too old to perform, he was replaced on the show by his son *Enzo*. Together, the two appeared in the feature film *My Dog Skip*, with Kevin Bacon. Moose passed away in 2006 at the age of 16.

And Then There Was Wishbone . . .

Children are still the biggest fans of a mischievous Russell named Wishbone, the star of the PBS series of the same name. The series debuted in 1995. In each episode, Wishbone leaps into another adventure with his human owner, Joe Talbot. Wishbone imagines himself as the hero in a classic novel and invites his audience to tag along on his madcap adventures, which include defeating the sheriff of Nottingham, journeying to the center of the Earth, confronting the Headless Horseman, tracking down the hound of the Baskervilles, and falling in love with the lovely Juliet. Viewers were hooked immediately and *Wishbone* became an instant success, winning four Emmy awards and one Peabody for its canine star. Wishbone has appeared in

People Magazine and on *The Tonight Show,* and has been a "category" on the game show, *Jeopardy!* Wishbone has, in fact, spawned a merchandise empire! The television series also inspired several book series. Currently, there are more than 50 books featuring Wishbone, which were published even after the TV series ended in 1998.

The Russell and Celebrities

Possibly because of his exposure in the media and his small size, the Russell has been one of the more popular pets of choice among celebrities. Among proud owners are singer Mariah Carey, whose pooch *Jack* is always at her side; actress/singer Bette Midler, ex-Beatle Paul McCartney, actress Goldie Hawn, and Britain's Prince Charles. Pop star Lindsay Lohan is the mom of *Brooklyn* and *Dakota*. Meanwhile, Olympic and world diving star Greg Louganis competes in top-level agility tests with his Russells, and has won many awards.

Breed Truths

Despite how wonderfully the Russell seems to adapt to the world of entertainment, it would be a big mistake for the potential owner to think this behavior comes naturally. It does not, and it requires intense training. For every effortless-looking scene on camera, hours of behind-the-scenes work were needed to get the right shot. The fact that the Russell is innately an extremely intelligent breed makes him a good candidate for television and films, because once properly trained, he is extremely responsive. But do not bring a Russell into your life believing that as soon as he enters your living room he will turn into an Eddie clone. Although your Russell has great potential, it will take determined effort and tireless patience on your part to help him become the great companion dog he was meant to be.

Characteristics

Russells like Eddie, Milo, and Wishbone are so adorable that children as well as adults automatically want one. To fanciers of the breed, the excellent qualities of the dog are readily apparent, but clearly, they are not a breed for everyone.

The Russell is a big dog in a little body. Compared with the pedigreed fox terriers of today, he is more akin to the original working dog of a century ago—bred to hunt and go to ground—who has an iron will and a need for strong training. It is the working structure, brain, and heart of the Russell that gives him an awesome character, an athleticism rivaled by none, and the versatility that makes him a great pet and companion.

Ideally, the Russell should always look alert and ready for his next challenge. He must appear quick-witted and confident, never timid or weak. He should also be energetic and friendly, never aggressive or nervous. In appearance, he is a small, predominately white-bodied dog with black and/or brown markings. His coat can be smooth or broken.

Chapter Two

The Mind of a Parson Russell Terrier

No doubt, you've heard the old adage "A mind is a terrible thing to waste." In the dog world, nowhere is this more applicable than to a Parson Russell Terrier, a dog whose natural intelligence can be the bliss or the bane of his existence. It all depends on you, his master, and how well you allow his mind to be developed.

Anyone who has ever owned a pet has probably spent a good deal of time wondering what his favorite companion was thinking. "If only my dog could talk" seems to be a common refrain, echoed by many perplexed human masters. But in truth, most animals are fairly effective communicators; humans simply need to learn to read the signs.

The Russell is particularly adept at making his desires known. This is not surprising and a throwback to his breed imperative as a working terrier. Today's Russell is extremely focused on what he wants, and when you don't listen or pay attention, he becomes frustrated. Sound familiar? When the Russell sits or stands at attention, looking you straight in the eyes; when he stretches forward, inclining his rear upward, and tilts his head toward you; when he leaps up, twirling in the air like a canine version of Cirque du Soleil, you can rest assured there is only one thing on his mind, and you can almost hear him verbalize it: *Gimme something to do, will ya, before I get into trouble?!*

The Russell is always looking for action. Whether it's a game of ball or walking with you to get the mail, he wants and needs to be busy. The more you give him to do, the better he'll appreciate and even look forward to his rest periods later on. Like many of

Breed Needs

The most common reason for behavioral problems in a Russell is lack of mental and physical activity. The Russell needs to be engaged in work and play that will challenge his mind and spirit. Ignoring him or leaving him to his own devices will result in a frustrated animal whose pent-up energy will explode in disruptive behavior.

his human counterparts, the Russell enjoys having a schedule. It's something his mind can readily process and eagerly anticipate. It's a good idea to allow your Russell to tag along as you do routine chores around the house like making the bed, loading the dishwasher, and gathering newspapers. For each new chore you do, give him a new command to learn. For example, when you start to sweep the kitchen floor, teach him to fetch the dustpan. Soon, you'll notice that he has become so used to the routine, he'll know what's expected of him at each juncture, and he'll be happy because he's doing what he was bred to do—work alongside his master!

What to Expect

The Russell is the "Roadrunner" of the canine world. Like that famous cartoon character, a Russell in action resembles a speeding bullet. Part of his charm is his seemingly boundless energy coupled with an almost impish enthusiasm. He plays hard and really enjoys himself. It's not unusual to observe a Russell having a blast all by himself. He'll run circles around a room, then put the brakes on, fix you with a mischievous grin, and resume with equal speed in the opposite direction. He loves to be a clown and the life of the party. Lacking a party, he'll make his own and have everyone around him in stitches. He's such an amusing character that people fall in love with him immediately. What the novice prospective owner fails to realize is that, without discipline, the Russell will take over, making an intolerable situation for both dog and master. Once the Russell takes a notion to do something, it will take hard training to break him of the habit, because at his core, he is very strong willed and unlikely to back down, which is also a throwback to his genetic pool.

Fun Facts

One Russell owner reports that every morning, she tells her dog what she has to do for the day and that he seems to know exactly which activities will involve him and which will not. For example, when she tells him it's time for their walk, he goes to the door and waits to be leashed; when she says it's time for lunch, he follows her into the kitchen and sits by his bowl. However, when she tells him she's going visit Margie, her sister, the dog makes an about-face and curls up in his bed for a nap!

Although the Russell is fearless, he is also the *bon vivant* of the dog world. He loves life, enjoys a good time, and is most content when he can share it with his humans. He has a passionate devotion to his people, to the extent that he would willingly lay down his life for them. However, the very traits that make him such a phenomenal companion can also be his undoing, if he has not been trained to marshal them in a positive way. The Russell has a "ready for anything" attitude. He's not easily intimidated, and he's always ready for a new adventure. It's up to the owner to make sure he's not biting off

more than he can chew. Remember, your Russell really thinks he's as big as a Mastiff, and that can get him into trouble if you're not vigilant.

It's impossible to discuss the Russell without marveling at his natural intelligence and ability to problem-solve, the true mark of superior intellect. From his beginnings, the Russell had to develop the ability to think quickly in order to outmaneuver the fox, not an easy task to be sure. The extent to which he was able to perform this function made him more valuable to the hunter. Added to this was his extraordinary staying power and utter relentlessness when it came to flushing out his prey, whether above or below ground. Such work demanded a feisty, goal-oriented little dog with an iron will and the smarts to persevere.

Breed Truths

To appreciate and understand the modern Russell temperament, it is essential to bear in mind that he was originally bred to be fearless, alert, tireless, and aggressive in the chase. The dog that has evolved into today's house pet still retains these traits, which, when properly channeled, make him an extremely loyal, protective, and lively companion.

None of this is lost on the Russell as we know him today. But although he has an exceptional ability to learn, he is also one of the most difficult breeds to train, simply because he is so smart and has a mind of his own. It is here that respect between dog and owner must come into play. It is not necessary to break an animal's spirit to teach him obedience. In the case of the Russell, who is innately one of the most intelligent breeds, such tactics would be an affront. The Russell needs to respect his master out of love, not fear. An animal who obeys out of fear is a loose cannon ready to blast the hand that administered the blow.

Common Misconceptions

It's practically impossible to look at a Russell pup and not fall in love. It's doubly impossible not to take that same baby home with you. After that, the real "fun" begins. If you've done your homework, you know that raising a Russell is a challenge, but one that will reward you tenfold if you stick to the program. On the other hand, if you bought your Russell expecting him to be a reincarnation of Eddie or Wishbone, you'll be in for a shock. There are many fallacies associated with this breed, and unfortunately the most often cited emanate from his appearance. Just remember what your mother told you about your first boyfriend: *Looks are often deceiving.* Nowhere is this truer than with the Russell.

The Russell is his own "person"—a true and independent spirit capable of living life to the fullest, with joy, exuberance, and a zest few canines can match. When he and his human master function as a team, the bond between them is unshakable and ownership is a privilege. But like all good things, it takes time, patience, and a lot of love to get there. Once you do, you won't find a better life companion than your boy *Jack*!

Helpful Hints

Be able to recognize the difference between high energy and nervousness. The Russell should never be anxious or upset, but curious and alert in demeanor. Although he is always on the move, he should not pace or become unduly concerned in any situation. Nor should he be overly aggressive toward other dogs or humans. Dogs who exhibit these undesirable characteristics should be professionally evaluated before the behavior becomes routine.

Behavior

The Russell is a happy, friendly dog who loves to be noticed, and will persevere until he gets his master's attention. He can also be very assertive, particularly in play, because he has a competitive spirit and loves to win. Overly assertive behavior, however, needs to be corrected from puppyhood or it could turn into aggressive behavior later on.

The Russell hates to be left alone. If every member of the family is regularly out all day, it can lead to a frustrated Russell, which in turn sets the stage for unwanted and often destructive behavior. For this reason, a Russell is not the best choice of pet for owners who work away from home. Sadly, this is one of the main reasons Russells are given up by owners who were not aware of the breed's needs before buying the dog.

Even if you are the perfect Russell owner, expect the path to doggy nirvana to be fraught with some labyrinthine twists and turns. But if you are patient and consistent, you and your boy will prevail. Because he was originally bred as a working terrier, the Russell can have behavioral issues that need to be addressed early on and corrected immediately. It's important to be able to identify the problem and its source. Only then can you deal with it logically, quickly, and effectively.

Breed Truths

Above all, the Russell wants to make his master happy. Once he realizes what you expect of him, he's smart enough to deliver. It gives him a sense of purpose and contentment. It means he's doing his job, and nothing makes a Russell happier than that!

Common Behavioral Issues

Most behavioral problems in the Russell stem from the same cause: lack of physical and mental stimulation. Although this may sound like an oversimplification, one only needs to remember that the Russell was bred to be a working hunter, and it makes perfect sense. Consequently, he is happiest when engaged in activity—*any* activity! But be forewarned: A quick walk around the block won't do. This is a breed used to spending long, hard hours traversing

BE PREPARED! Common Russell Misconceptions

Misconception	Truth
Small size = lapdog	A thousand times NO! The Russell is not a couch potato, and any attempt to turn him into one will prove frustrating to both the dog and the owner.
Easy to train	Smart, yes, but training can be challenging because the Russell has a mind of his own and an iron will.
Laid-back	Not a chance! The Russell is not content to sit around and do nothing. He's a dog on the move and must always have stimulating activity.
Quiet	Wrong again! The Russell was bred to bay and bark to flush out prey. This dog will sound the alarm when a pin drops!
Timid	*Hello!?* The Russell thinks he's the dog version of Muhammad Ali! He is fiercely protective and has no fear, and that often gets him into trouble.
Non-athletic = does not require exercise	Major mistake! Set your new Russell down on your living room floor and watch Mr. Energizer Pup go. This boy will *never* run out of battery life. He needs *extreme* exercise, so better get your running shoes ready.
Condo dog	Not unless you plan long, daily trips to a nearby dog park! The Russell is a country boy at heart. He needs space, preferably his own fenced yard.
I just bought Eddie.	*You wish!* Remember, it took long, hard hours of professional training and handling to make Eddie into a TV dog. The Russell is not the way he is portrayed on TV or in films.

extremely rough terrain and then burrowing underground to corner prey. Even though today's Russell does not have the same opportunities or imperatives as his ancestors before him, his instinct as a working terrier remains intact. Thus, his boundless energy needs a positive outlet. Lacking one, he will simply find other ways to burn up all that adrenaline. Invariably, that spells T-R-O-U-B-L-E and sets the stage for unwanted behavior to take hold.

Separation Anxiety One of the most common explanations for unwanted behavior is separation anxiety. It happens with both puppies and adult dogs. When you bring a puppy into the house, you separate him from his littermates. It's usual for him to be lonely for his playmates and express that by

whining and crying. When you replace his littermates with his new human family, you create a new pack for him. Consequently, when he's left home alone, because members of the family work, go to school, or just go out for a time, he will cry and whine, and may even exhibit destructive behavior in the form of chewing on furniture, digging up carpets, and shredding cushions.

He's not being deliberately destructive or punishing you for going out; he's merely acting out his fear that you may not return. The best way to assuage that fear is to take some preliminary steps before leaving him.

Breed Needs

- Take your pup for a long walk before you leave him alone, so he can both relieve himself and get some exercise.
- Leave your pup in a secure place, preferably a crate where he has room to stand and move around reasonably well.
- Place safe toys and chews in the crate so he can amuse himself while you're gone.

The best way to make your Russell a well-behaved member of the family is to provide him with the mental and physical activity necessary to meet the needs of his dynamic personality. Plan for at least one fairly rigorous daily exercise regimen for your boy. Remember, a bored Russell is a recipe for disaster.

- Leave a CD on with soft music playing.
- After you put your puppy into his crate, spend a few minutes going about your normal routine. In other words, don't make a big deal out of your impending departure. Then quietly go to the door and leave.

Helpful Hints

Don't say good-bye to your pup before you leave the house. Don't throw him doggy kisses, as that will alert him to the fact that you're going away. Just go. If you've already crate-trained your Russell, he'll usually just amuse himself with his toys for a while and then fall asleep.

Adult dogs can also suffer from separation anxiety, and in many cases, it is the owner who initially sets the stage for this type of phobic behavior. Humans tend to lavish a great deal of affection on their pets, which is a good thing. However, some outbursts of affection, particularly when you are about to leave the house, can have the opposite effect on the dog and create an anxiety situation.

Consider it from the dog's point of view: One minute you're hugging, petting, and kissing him, and the next minute you're walking out the door. The dog is alone—no more hugs and kisses, just alone. He's deprived of affection and the affection giver as well. Why wouldn't he become anxious? He's afraid you'll never return! So he acts out a classic anxiety response: He paces, he cries, he digs, he tears things. Why? Because he's trying to get out of the house and find you! And the more he can't get through those walls and doors, the more his panic escalates, even to the point of causing him to lose bodily control and soil the floors.

When you return home and find chaos, your first impulse will be to yell at the dog and punish him. That is the worst possible thing to do, because then you create a *Catch-22* situation. The dog made the mess because he misses you and is trying to be reunited with you. If you punish him, he will also dread your return and be anxious about that as well. It then becomes an all-around no-win situation.

CHECKLIST

The best way to allay separation anxiety in the adult dog is through consistent conditioning and training. Never yell at him or punish him. Instead, focus on providing an atmosphere that will reduce his anxiety.

- ✔ Provide him with a comfortable place to stay, such as a bed or mat.
- ✔ Handle his toys and chews, so they will have your scent, then place them on his mat.
- ✔ Leave a radio or CD player on.

Before leaving, take your Russell for a walk. Again, don't make a big deal out of your imminent departure. Act normally. Pay no special attention to the dog. Then leave the house quietly without saying good-bye. First, stay out of the house for a few minutes and return. The next time, extend your time away, gradually working up to being able to leave your Russell for longer periods of time. When you come home, don't pay any attention to him. After a few minutes, call him over. If he obeys, reward him with praise and a treat. This type of consistent conditioning should relieve his anxiety and eventually allow you to leave the house without worry.

Some dogs exhibit severe separation anxiety, no matter what you do. In these cases, you can opt to try doggy day care. If that doesn't work, it is advisable to seek professional intervention from an animal behaviorist. Medications to calm your dog may be prescribed but should be used only as a last resort and only under the direction of a veterinarian.

CAUTION

Always keep in mind that yelling or screaming at your dog will not correct unwanted behavior. Quite the opposite. It will only raise your blood pressure and confuse or frighten your pet. In most instances, your dog doesn't realize he's done something wrong. It's your job to communicate that to him in a way he will understand. Your Russell wants to please you, so he will be eager to learn how to do that.

Other Fear-Related Phobias Some dogs exhibit fear-related responses to external stimuli such as loud noises, fireworks, or thunder. Usually as the puppy matures, he will grow out of this and habituate. But in some cases, adult dogs will continue to react adversely. What makes the situation worse and even contributes to the animal's fear is the human owner's attempt to comfort him. This makes the dog even more fearful and a vicious cycle begins. Instead, if your dog exhibits a fear reaction, act completely indifferent. Do not acknowledge the dog at all. This may seem cruel, but it is just the opposite. When you act normally, your Russell will get the idea that there is nothing wrong. Once you identify the cause of his fear, you can follow a stepped progression targeted at desensitizing him to the stimuli.

Willfulness/Stubbornness
Russells naturally think that their way is the best and indeed, the only way. This can be very frustrating to

Helpful Hints

A dog exhibiting willful or stubborn behavior is begging you to notice him. If you yell and scream at him or keep repeating a command, he's getting exactly what he wants—your undivided attention. He hasn't earned that yet, so don't give it to him. Instead, turn your back on him and ignore him. Wait a few moments. Then, without turning toward him, give him a command: *"Jack, come."* In most cases, the dog will obey. When he does, acknowledge him by praising him. When he realizes that he doesn't get attention for one type of behavior, in this case willfulness, he will soon reject that behavior in favor of the new behavior, obeying your command, because then he gets what he wants—and so do you!

the owner. For example, you give your Russell a command: *"Jack, drop the shoe."* He ignores you. You repeat the command, this time in a louder voice. He ignores you again. Finally, you scream the command at the top of your lungs, and not only does he ignore you, but he begins flailing the shoe in the air as if in a frenzy. At this point, many a frustrated owner will angrily go up to the dog and grab the other end of the object and start pulling it, trying to wrench it away from him. But this only makes Jack pull harder. Is he being obstinate, willful, or stubborn? Yes, to all of the above, but now he also thinks this is a game: *Tug-of-war— what fun! Let's keep on playing*! As you keep pulling and screaming, Jack is having the time of his life.

Barking All dogs bark. It's one of the ways they communicate. Most barking is perfectly acceptable. For example, your dog will bark for four basic reasons: He has to go out to relieve himself; he's alerting you to a situation, such as someone coming up the driveway; or he's hungry; he sees another dog and is in effect saying "Hi." This is considered normal barking. Nuisance barking is another matter.

Helpful Hints

If your Russell barks sporadically for prolonged periods, it's likely he's bored. If he does this while you are at home, try distracting him with an interesting toy. If he barks while you're out of the house, make sure you give him a good walk before you go and leave him with plenty of toys to keep him busy while you're gone. If he still barks while you're away, he is probably suffering from separation anxiety.

Whenever your dog barks continuously for no apparent reason, it's a nuisance. More than most breeds, the Russell is very vocal. Again, it's part of his genetic makeup. His ancestors were bred to bark and bay loudly and nonstop, so the hunter could locate the dog and the prey he cornered, often underground. Although most of today's pet Russell's will never get to bay at a fox, it doesn't stop them from using those high-pitched vocals to the chagrin of anyone who is unlucky enough to be within hearing range.

CAUTION

Your Russell is perfectly capable of digging his way out of a homemade backyard fence, so be sure your fence is professionally installed. You might want to ask the installer to provide a tension wire and a concrete base all around the perimeter of the fence as an extra safety measure.

Chewing Dogs love to chew. Puppies chew because they're teething; adult dogs chew because they like the way it feels. The object is to keep Jack from chewing things like your shoes and the furniture. The best way is to provide your dog with safe, tasty chew toys such as Nylabones and rawhide treats. But, if he still grabs your slipper, don't yell at him. Distract him with one of his toys and when he takes the toy, praise him.

Digging Many dogs dig when they're outdoors. It's a normal canine activity. There are many reasons for this: Maybe your boy smells a rabbit or

FYI: The Dig Zone

Set aside a neutral zone in your yard where your Russell can dig to his heart's content. Devise a game of hide-and-seek by burying some of your dog's toys or treats. The next time you catch your boy digging in a forbidden area, go over to him and say, *"No dig"* or just *"No"* in a firm voice, then physically take him away and bring him over to his neutral zone.

As he starts to sniff the ground and dig up the treats you've buried, praise him. Each day bury a few new treats or toys. Take your Russell to the designated area and encourage him to find the objects, praising him each time he does. You'll be amazed at how quickly he'll catch on and what a great time he'll have digging in his approved area.

a possum; maybe he just wants to bury a toy or a bone. If it's hot, he may dig a hole and then sit in it to cool off. Not surprisingly, Russells love to dig, anything and everything. It's a throwback to his heritage. Although your boy is not apt to find a fox or a badger hiding in the holes and tunnels he's dug all over the yard, he's still in doggy heaven. You, on the other hand, are ready to wring his little neck. Instead of trying to eradicate a behavior that comes naturally to this breed, come up with a compromise you both can live with, like his own dig area.

Chasing Most dogs like to chase. But in the case of the Russell, it's more of a breed imperative than a casual fancy. Terriers were bred to give chase and flush creatures out of their holes. The Russell, in particular, will run after anything that moves, including other animals, cars, and people. Russells are famous for taking off after an object of interest and disappearing, sometimes for hours or even days. This can be both frustrating for the owner and dangerous for the dog, especially if you live near high-traffic areas. The only way to nip this problem in the bud is to teach your Russell the *no* command early on. However, no matter how well trained he is, don't ever rely on training to override instinct. Jack may love you to death and be obedient to a fault, but the sight of a cat dashing across a street is too powerful a stimulus. It completely changes his focus, and in a flash, he's chasing after it. All your screams for him to come back will fall on deaf ears. Does this mean you shouldn't bother to obedience-train your Russell? Not at all. You should just be aware that training does not preclude the necessity to exercise commonsense safety measures. Always take precautions to ensure your dog's safety when he's out of the house and yard area by leash walking him. Do not ever let him off his leash in public places and trust that training alone will keep him out of harm's way.

Aggression The Russell tends to be aggressive, particularly with other dogs of the same sex. This type of aggression is endemic to the breed. For this reason it is advisable *not* to have two Russells of the same sex in a household.

The Russell can also be aggressive toward other small pets like cats, rabbits, and rodents. Puppies are naturally rough and aggressive with their litter-mates. Thus, when you bring your Russell pup home, he may play bite, snarl, mouth and nip at your hands, because to him playing with his new owner is no different from playing with his littermates. It's up to you to draw the line when his play becomes too rough.

Whereas aggressive behavior in puppies is relatively simple to control, it's more difficult in the adult Russell. Adult dog aggression can involve mounting, push-ing, growling, barking, and baring teeth. One of the best ways to deal with this type of aggression is to obedience-train your dog and to teach him that you, not he, is the head of the household. Never try to stare down an aggressive dog. In the dog's mind, this is a cue for a confronta-tion. It tells him you want to fight.

Helpful Hints

The best way to distract your Russell from unwanted behavior is to use diversionary tactics to make him cease and desist. Use a whistle, a rattle, a squeaky toy, or whatever innovation you can muster, so long as it gets his attention. Once you have his attention, immediately give him a command: "*Jack, come.*" When he comes, praise him and give him a treat.

Adult dogs may also exhibit dominance aggression, which means they want their own way. If your Russell growls or snaps when you attempt to move him off a sofa or put him out in the yard, he is basically challenging you: *Go on, make me do it*. If an owner establishes himself as the pack leader from the moment the dog becomes a part of the family unit, this behavior will never happen. Unfortunately, the Russell who has not been well trained is far more predisposed to dominance-related aggression than most breeds.

Use the following tactics to break a pattern of dominance-related aggression:

- Deprive your Russell of affection and treats for several hours.
- Call your Russell and give him a command: *"Jack, sit."*
- If your Russell responds, give him lots of affection and a treat.
- Repeat this several times during the day.
- Reward your Russell *only* if he obeys.

By the end of the day, you will have conditioned your dog to obey on *your* terms. His reward is that he gets what he wants: affection and food! At the same time, the Russell is reminded of his subordinate role in the pack.

Mounting   Owners are always embarrassed when their dogs display mounting behavior because they assume it's sexually motivated. This isn't usually the case. Dogs mount other dogs to show control or dominance. Similarly, if your dog mounts a human, he is trying to establish dominance. This type of mounting is a form of aggressive behavior and must be corrected immediately. If you observe your Russell engaging in mounting either with you or someone else, say *"Off"* in a stern voice and push him off. The next time he tries to mount, turn and walk away. Your boy will soon get the message.

CAUTION

Some dogs growl if you go near their food. If your Russell exhibits this behavior, walk away and then call him over. When he comes, reward him with praise and a treat. This will allow him to make a pleasant, nonthreatening association between you and his food.

However, for some dogs, behavior modification will require professional intervention. In extreme cases, medication may be recommended. Never medicate your dog for any reason without first consulting with your veterinarian.

Eating Feces   Like mounting, feces eating is especially embarrassing to humans. There's no clear-cut reason why dogs seem to enjoy eating their own waste or that of other dogs. Some schools of thought theorize that dogs eat feces to supplement nutritional deficiencies in their diets. However, if you are feeding your boy a high-quality dog food, this isn't very likely. In the case of puppies who are left confined in crates for a long period of time, feces eating can be attributed to boredom. If you have to be away for a long part of the day, don't crate your puppy. Instead, cordon off a section of the kitchen that you've already puppy-proofed, and provide a "potty" area for him far away from his bedding and teach him to eliminate there. If you also provide plenty of safe toys for him to play with so he won't get bored, there will be less chance of him eating his feces. The best prevention is to pick up any fecal matter before your pup has a chance to reach it.

Is Your Russell Stressed Out?

The dictates of the modern world have made stress an accepted part of daily life. Today, physicians see more stress-related illnesses than ever before. But humans are not the only ones susceptible. Our pets are also showing signs of stress. That's hardly surprising since the accelerated pace of our lives cannot help but filter down to our canine companions. The Russell is even more susceptible than most because he is so in tune with his human family that he picks up on their emotions and reacts accordingly. Being left alone for too long, bringing a new pet in the home, moving to a different home, loud noises, and thunderstorms are other things can also contribute to his increased stress level. Some of the ways you can tell if your boy is stressed out are changes in his behavior and eating patterns, digestive distress, and depression. Like overly stressed humans, your Russell can also suffer from hypertension!

Helpful Hints

If your puppy's play becomes too intense, tell him, "*No*" firmly and then stop playing with him. Once he has calmed down, start playing with him again. If he gets nippy, repeat the word "*No*," stop playing again, let him rest, and then resume play. Soon, he'll get the message and know just how far he is allowed to go.

If you suspect your boy may be experiencing too much stress, help him and yourself to unwind by playing soothing music or the sounds of ocean waves. Many studies have been done documenting the therapeutic effect that music has on our pets—even the sounds that seem to work best. Dogs apparently prefer classical music and will become so relaxed after listening for just a few moments that they will stop stressful behavior and slip into a sound sleep. There are pet relaxation CDs available, including one from Tom Nazziola called *Music My Pet, Classical Cuts*. Check it out.

The Russell Senses

Even though humans and canines have the same five senses in common, dogs depend on their senses more than humans do to appraise their surroundings. Consequently, a dog's senses are far more acute than those of humans. The Russell, in particular, because of his heritage as a working terrier, has more highly developed senses than most breeds. A working terrier bred to go to ground had to be able to sniff out quarry burrowed often many feet underground!

The Sense of Smell

Try calling your Russell from a far distance. He will probably respond to your voice immediately by looking in your direction. But he will hesitate to move until you get closer. This is because he is waiting to pick up your scent to make sure it's really you! By far, the Russell's strongest sense is that of smell. A dog has approximately 40 times as many scent receptors as humans. Dogs use their sense of smell to alert them to a variety of situations like imminent danger or the proximity of another dog. They are adept at following scent paths and identifying different scents. For this reason, dogs are trained to work with law enforcement agencies to detect drugs, bombs, dead bodies, and to help find missing people.

Fun Facts

A dog's nose has approximately 200 million scent receptors compared with about 5 million in a human! Dogs bred for tracking and hunting have even more. The longer the dog's nose, the more scent receptors it has and the better it can smell.

The Sense of Hearing

The Russell has an astoundingly good sense of hearing. You'll notice that he will alert you to someone outside the house long before that person gets to the front door. Dogs can hear over many more frequencies than humans. The combination of acute smell and hearing is the reason that many dogs are used for guard duty and protection.

Fun Facts

According to several studies, dogs prefer listening to the German composer Bach and actually bark less when listening to his music!

The Sense of Sight

Unlike humans, dogs trust their sense of sight the least. Your Russell is not able to distinguish colors as well as you are, and for this reason he depends more on his sense of smell than his sense of sight. However, he has an exceptional ability to detect movement in the darkness, unlike humans. This skill was, no doubt, important to the working terrier of old who had to navigate dark underground tunnels to perform his job.

The Sense of Touch

Dogs also have a superior sense of touch. Your Russell's entire body is covered with extremely sensitive nerve endings. Rub or pet him on practically any spot and he'll respond. This is one of the reasons dogs love to be petted and touched. It just feels so good!

The Sense of Taste

We humans enjoy our food because of the way it tastes. Dogs don't taste things as strongly as we do. When you offer your Russell either his meal or a treat, he'll sniff at it first. That's because he identifies his like or dislike for the food based on its smell. If he likes the smell, then he'll eat it.

Body Language

Long before humans took the notion to communicate with canines, they were communicating among themselves for thousands of years with no problem. The system they used was relatively rudimentary: biting and growling. Today, dogs still communicate through growling and other physical contact. Dogs learn body language from their mothers by the time they are eight weeks old and use it on their littermates.

Fun Facts

People often swear that dogs have a so-called "sixth sense" because they seem to have a heightened ability to detect such things as weather and climate fluctuations; changes in the earth's magnetic field that cause tornados, earthquakes, and so on; and even the moods of his master!

Breed Truths

Dogs "smile" showing their teeth only to humans, not to other dogs!

PERSONALITY POINTERS

Parson Russell Terrier Body Language

Russell Mood	Friendly	Curious or Excited	Playful
Head Carriage	Normal posture and head position	Normal posture and head position	"Play bow," chest and head lowered to ground, head looking up
Eyes	Wide open	Wide open	Wide open
Ears	Alert, forward	Alert, forward	Alert, forward
Mouth	Closed or relaxed and slightly open in a "smile"	Mouth open, teeth covered with lips, may pant	Closed or slightly open
Body	Relaxed posture or wiggling with excitement	Relaxed posture or wriggling with excitement	Chest lowered to ground, rump elevated
Tail	Wagging	Wagging	Wagging

Face Although a dog's face is not nearly as expressive as a human face because dogs have fewer facial muscles, your Russell still uses his face to convey emotions. If he wrinkles his forehead, he's telling you that he's confused; if he also tilts his head or raises his eyes quizzically, he's asking you for a little more information.

Eyes Dogs are able to use their eyes to convey a gamut of emotions from happiness to fear to downright anger. When your Russell's eyes brighten, he either wants to play or he sees something that he likes, such as a new toy or a doggy pal. However, if he's frightened, his pupils will dilate and you'll be able to see the whites of his eyes quite clearly. If he averts his eyes, he's trying to avoid a confrontation. On the other hand, if he's got his dander up and ready to meet his opponent head-on, his eyes will narrow and follow every move of the object of his ire.

Lips, Teeth, Tongue Dogs use their mouth apparatus quite effectively to signal a variety of moods.

CAUTION

If a dog looks at you using angry body language, never look him back in the eye. He will perceive this as a challenge to defend his position.

Apprehensive or Anxious	Fearful	Subordinate
Neck stiff, head may be pulled back slightly	Head slightly lowered	Head slightly lowered
Wide open, may appear "bug-eyed," whites of eyes may show, may have fixed stare	Eyes wide, whites of eyes may show	Eyes partially closed
Pulled back	Ears pulled back or flattened against skull	Ears flattened against skull
Closed or slightly open in a tight "grin" with teeth showing	Slightly open, teeth may be visible, may be drooling	Lips of mouth pulled back in "grin," may lick or nuzzle
	Tense, trembling, may take up on a position poised to run, may release anal sac contents in fear	May roll over on back and expose belly, may also dribble urine in submission
Partially lowered	Lowered between legs	Lowered between legs

If your Russell wants something, or if he's happy or just feels like having some fun, he will often pull his lips back in what appears to be a smile. However, if he bares *clenched* teeth and wrinkles his nose, then he's ready to attack.

Ears Dogs can locate the origin of a sound in $\frac{6}{100}$th of a second! Because a dog's sense of hearing is so acute, he is able to move his ears to follow sounds. If your Russell raises his ears, he's either relaxed, listening for something, or showing acceptance of a situation. On the other hand, if his ears go back, he is showing either submission or fear.

Tail Everyone loves a tail-wagging dog! It signals that he is happy and ready to play. But when your Russell tucks his tail between his legs, he's being submissive. A dog also uses his tail for balance. Thus, if he holds his tail down rigidly, he may be getting ready to jump.

Voice All dogs are vocal, and Russells are more vocal than most. The pitch or volume of his bark, whine, or whimper increases with the intensity of his emotion. His bark can be playful or aggressive.

Your Russell's stance is important and is a generally good indicator of his emotional state at any given time. The following are some common Russell postures and their interpretation:

- Normal: head held high, alert, jaw relaxed, tail moving freely
- Submission: crouching, ears back, tail down
- Dominance aggression: teeth bared, ears forward, direct eye contact, confident advance with tail wagging slowly
- Fear aggression: body tense, tail rigid, teeth bared, ears drawn back, hair on his back standing on end, growling
- Ready for play: front legs crouching into a "bow" with haunches raised, head held high, tail wagging

Avoiding Mixed Messages

Despite our best intentions, we humans still end up sending our dogs mixed messages. How? Simple: We are inconsistent about the way we want our dog to

Helpful Hints

If your dog jumps on you when you come home, don't punish him. He's just greeting you. Instead teach him how you want him to behave, then give him loads of love.

FYI: The Doggy Dance

A dog's posture or stance is also an indicator of what he's feeling. If you have ever observed two unleashed dogs meeting, you will notice how they circle and sniff each other. This "doggy dance" is actually the way they size each other up, exchange information, and determine whether the meeting will be a pleasant *hello* or a confrontation. If one dog places his head on the other's neck or shoulder, he is signaling dominance. If the other dog lies down, and begins to turn, exposing his belly, it means he's accepting of the situation. In that case, the dominant dog may urinate and go off on his merry way and a confrontation is avoided.

behave. Behavior that is allowed on one day is forbidden the next. The result is a very confused pet and an equally unhappy owner.

Case in point: When you first brought your Russell puppy home and he jumped up and down, jumped on and off your lap, licked your face, and mouthed your wrist, you thought it was cute. You hugged, kissed, and cuddled him in response. You probably even encouraged him to keep it up. A year down the road, Jack is still jumping, licking, and mouthing. Only now, it's not so cute and you reprimand him. A behavior that used to be rewarded with a lot of petting and cuddling is suddenly met with yelling, screaming, pushing, and angry looks. What's a dog to think?

To avoid this type of confusion, it's important to distinguish acceptable behavior from unacceptable behavior, and enforce it. In other words, set ground rules. This way, your Russell will be clear about what's expected of him from the moment he comes into your household.

Make it easy on yourself and draw up a game plan. In a few sentences describe the behavioral goals you want to achieve with your Russell. Then make a list of the commands you will use to elicit each specific behavior from your dog. Post them in a conspicuous place, such as on the refrigerator door, and then stick to the plan! In all things, remember, consistency is the key!

Helpful Hints

Remember, always be consistent. Use the same words or "cues" with the same corresponding actions every time. And most important, don't talk up a blue streak. It'll only sound like meaningless jabber to your dog, and your boy Jack will tune you right out!

Communicating with Your Russell

Voice Since dogs first walked the earth, they have used their voices to convey a variety of emotions and information. Barks, growls, howls, whines, and whimpers are all a part of your dog's vocal repertoire when communicating with other dogs, and each means something different, depending on the specific sound and intonation. You've probably noticed with some amusement the broad range of vocalizations that come out of your Russell's mouth. Sometimes you wonder how he is even able to make some of the sounds that he does. From a strong bark that alerts you to a stranger approaching, to an almost sing-songy refrain when he's being his playful, mischievous self, not to mention the whole cacophony of sounds in between, your boy uses his voice to convey a message. Similarly, you can use intonations in your voice to communicate a message or command to your Russell. Because dogs are extremely sensitive to pitch, it's important that you use the same tone of voice each time you combine it with a verbal command; otherwise your Russell will become confused. By using a specific tone of voice in combination with a specific word or movement, you can greatly enhance your ability to get the message across. For example, when want to take your Russell out for a walk, use an enthusiastic happy tone: "Let's go, Jack!" Then your Russell will relate the up-tempo of your voice with the words, and going out will become a very positive thing to do.

Hands Combining hand signals with voice commands is one of the best ways to reinforce training. Hand signals are fairly easy for most dogs because they are very observant. Notice how your Russell will follow your every movement with his eyes. What he's doing is watching for a "cue" from you. Thus when you combine a verbal command like "Jack, *sit*" with a hand signal, your boy will have an easier time figuring out what you want. Most trainers teach hand signals simultaneously with verbal commands. Hand signals can also come in handy when friends or family try to communicate with your dog. Since tones of voice vary from one person to the next, using predetermined hand signals alone can avoid confusion. Furthermore, as your Russell ages, he could suffer from hearing loss. If he learned hand signals as a youngster, it will make your ability to communicate as easy and rich as ever.

Facial Expressions No doubt you've noticed how your Russell's expression changes as he listens to you. Whether it's a quizzical tilt of the head, lips pulled back in what you will swear is a smile, or a peculiar glint that seems to come into his eyes when he's ready for some fun, he uses his face and head to convey a mood, in very much the same way as you do. Although humans have a far greater range of facial expressions than dogs, you can combine a specific facial expression and tone of voice to convey a message to your dog. For example, smiling when your Russell obeys a command, combined with the phrase "Good boy" or "yes" in an enthusiastic, happy voice tells your boy that you are pleased. Conversely, if he's done something naughty, furrowing your brows or shaking your head while saying, "Bad boy" or "no" in a strident tone will convey the opposite message.

Body Movement

Dogs are masters in the use of body language. They use their bodies to greet other dogs, fend them off, play, fight, and establish dominance. When dogs who are friends meet, they will often jump on each other in a playful gesture. On the other hand, when a dog wants to establish dominance, he will bump the other dog or lean his head across the other dog's shoulders. Similarly, you can use body movement to communicate with your Russell. If you're pleased with him, you can stroke or pet him enthusiastically. If he's been bad, simply turn away from him.

Scents

Dogs can learn about their surroundings, other dogs, people, and just about anything through scents. All dogs have a highly developed sense of smell, and this is doubly true of the Russell because he was bred to rely on scents to locate and flush out quarry. Notice how much of your dog's time outdoors is spent with his nose to the ground, sniffing just about everything in sight. Different scents convey different information. When your Russell sniffs another's dog's urine, he can tell many things: the sex, proximity, and basic history of the other dog. Similarly, by combining a specific scent with a word or phrase, you can communicate a message to your Russell. When you're cooking, you use the smell of the food to tell your boy it's time to eat. When you want to leave the house for a stretch of hours, you can spray a certain scent, such as vanilla, by the door and tell your Russell you're going out for a while. Your Russell will catch on very quickly and soon make the association between a scent and a message you are trying to get across to him.

Chapter Three

How to Choose a Parson Russell Terrier

Once you've determined that the Parson Russell Terrier is the breed for you, the next step is to choose that special dog with whom you'll ideally share the next 15-plus years of your life. This will take quite a bit of time and research. Purchasing a dog is not like buying a car that you can trade in for a newer and better model whenever you grow tired of it. A dog is a living, feeling, and innocent creature. Buying one should never be an impulse decision or based on anything but compatibility and your willingness to take full responsibility for his well-being from the moment you bring him into your home. Some prospective pet owners think they can "try a dog out" for a period of time and then return him if for any reason they're not completely satisfied. Technically this is true. A reputable breeder will allow you to return a dog if you change your mind. Certainly there are some valid reasons why this could happen. But it is unfair to the dog to bring it into your home and your life under "false pretenses"—namely, that you did not do your homework and adequately assess your suitability for owning a pet before buying one. Thus, to avoid such an unpleasant situation, be sure you know all the pros and cons of pet ownership, especially those specific to the breed you choose. Several factors need to be taken into consideration before you make a decision. Keep in mind that just as no two people are exactly alike, no two dogs are alike. Though they may look similar, each has his own personality, even among a litter of adorable Russell puppies.

Parson Russell Terrier Choices

Before setting out to find your Russell, it's a good idea to take a few moments to reflect on what you are looking for in your new dog. Every person will have different requirements, and it's prudent to be as honest with yourself as possible. Start by making a list of characteristics you would like to find in your pet, ranging from personality traits to lifestyle imperatives and even looks. Write everything down and then when you begin to screen puppies, you can share your list with the breeder and together select the dog that will best suit your needs and expectations.

Male or Female?

One of the first considerations is whether you want a male or a female. Some people are partial to one sex over the other. Many owners feel that females are less independent than males, less likely to stray, and make better pets. Other owners swear that males are more constant and companionable than females. It really comes down to your own preference, if you have one. In general, males tend to be more aggressive and territorial than females, who can be less

Breed Truths

Parson Russell Terriers come in two coat types: smooth or broken. Each gives the dog a completely different look, so you'll have to decide which you prefer. Both coats shed, but a broken coat requires slightly more maintenance than a smooth coat.

defiant and more docile, though this is not always true, especially in the case of a Russell. You may also want to consider that it is a simpler procedure for

BE PREPARED! The Cost of Owning a Russell

Whether you choose a pet or a show puppy, you will have to bear the responsibility and cost of his day-to-day care for the rest of his life. A Russell puppy can cost anywhere from several hundred dollars to more than a thousand dollars, if purchased from a breeder, and depending on his pedigree. A puppy or adult Russell adopted from a shelter or rescue can cost between $75 and $300.

During your puppy's first year, he can cost anywhere from $600 to more than $5,000. After the first year, you can expect the annual tab for your Russell to look something like this:

- Food: $150–$500
- Veterinary Exams: $45–$200
- Vaccinations: $30–$150
- Worming and Fecal Exams: $20–$50
- Heartworm Treatment: $25–$130
- Grooming: $20–$400
- Training: $50–$500
- Supplies: $100–$300
- Miscellaneous: $200–$500
- Pet Insurance: $150–$500 annually, depending on plan and age of dog at inception

a veterinarian to neuter a male dog than to spay a female, which usually requires a longer hospitalization and post-op care.

Puppy or Adult?

Next you'll need to decide whether you want a puppy or an adult dog. Russell puppies are totally irresistible, but a puppy will also require more initial hands-on care than an adult dog, who will usually be housetrained and have some rudimentary training when you get him. Often the decision between getting a puppy or an adult depends on your lifestyle.

If you live in an apartment or condo without adequate space for a designated puppy play area, you might want to go for the older dog. Similarly, if you are out of the house most of the day or you have family responsibilities that keep you busy, you probably won't have time to devote to rearing a puppy. Remember that puppies need to be fed and taken out often. Unlike adult dogs, they need supervision most of the time. Puppies are naturally inquisitive and should never be left to their own devices, which can be both dangerous and destructive. They also need to be housetrained. If you don't have the time and the patience to do this, an older dog may work out better for you. If there are young children in the house, a well-mannered adult dog is probably a better choice because he will generally adapt to the environment more easily and tolerate more from a child than a puppy.

FYI: Exhibiting Expenses

The difference in price between show and pet puppies can be substantial, depending on the dog's pedigree. Further, showing your dog involves many additional expenses like hiring a professional handler if you will not be showing the dog yourself. If your dog will be traveling with his handler from show to show, as many dogs do, you'll also be expected to pay for food, board, grooming, and general care while he's away from home. Even if you plan to show your dog yourself, you'll have to enroll him in conformation training classes, where you will both learn the art of exhibiting. Showing your Russell also entails extra grooming costs. Every time he's entered into a show, you'll have to pay a registration fee. So, if you have no intention of exhibiting your Russell in AKC conformation shows, you might want to opt for a pet-quality dog. Pet-quality dogs can be entered in both obedience and agility trials, which have to do with performance rather than looks.

Keep in mind that if you plan to show your Russell in AKC conformation shows, he must be intact—he cannot be neutered until after you stop showing him.

Show Puppy or Pet Puppy?

Another thing you should consider is whether you want a pet or a show dog. If you would like to get into the sport of conformation showing, a puppy will be the better choice. Sometimes breeders also sell show-quality adults and adolescents whom they haven't had time to exhibit themselves, but want to place in a "show" family. If you want to show your dog, it's important to make that known to the breeder. Each litter is evaluated and separated into show and pet specimens. One is not better than the other. The difference between the show and the pet pups has to do with each

individual dog's strict conformation to the AKC standard. Generally, differences between pet and show puppies are so slight that only an experienced breeder can distinguish them. However, if you do plan to show your dog, become familiar with the AKC breed standard so that you can discuss the puppy choices more effectively with the breeder.

If, like most buyers, you're looking for a dog who will primarily become a member of your family and a lifetime companion, then a pet-quality puppy is the right choice. Remember, a pet-quality pup is in no way inferior to a show dog!

Keep in mind, too, that any emergency situations (and every dog owner has them) will require additional expenses. Multiply all of the above by the average lifespan of your Russell, which is about 15 years. Of course, you may spend more or less, but the point is, you must be ready, willing, and financially able to care for a Russell. Will he be worth it? That's up to you. Raising a Russell can be as trying as it is rewarding. The cost is not only about *money*, but more important, about *love*. So before you adopt a Russell make sure you have enough of both to keep him healthy and happy for his lifetime.

Choosing a Breeder

Once you have made some preliminary decisions about your future pup and your total ability to be a Russell owner, the next and most important step is to find a reputable breeder. First, a word of caution: Practically anyone who has a litter of puppies for sale can call himself a "breeder." Such breeders can even produce AKC papers, which prove only that both the sire and dam are AKC registered. There is more to breeding than putting a male and a female together. It is a science that requires both knowledge and experience. If you feel that this type of breeder doesn't have adequate knowledge or experience, you should avoid purchasing a puppy, or at least thoroughly investigate before doing so.

CAUTION

Impulse Buying

If you have contacted several breeders and none of them have puppies immediately available, do not, in your haste, go to your local pet store and buy a puppy without some investigating. Avoid impulse buying unless you are prepared to deal with the consequences later. If you totally fall in love with a pet store pup, find out as much information from the pet store as possible about the sire and dam. Some pet stores are more reputable than others and keep better records of the puppy's background. Then take him to your veterinarian for an immediate evaluation. If you want a dog right away, you may also want to consider adopting a rescue Russell.

Fortunately, there are many good breeders dedicated to preserving and promoting the integrity of the breed. This means that they have breeding programs that are committed as much as possible to producing litters of puppies that are structurally sound, healthy, and free of genetic defects. Furthermore, don't be surprised if you call a breeder and are told no puppies are available, but that reservations are being taken for a future litter. The reason is that reputable breeders produce only a few litters per year—some produce only one litter a year, others even fewer than that. Unlike puppy mills, which turn out litter after litter for a profit, a conscientious breeder is not in the business of selling puppies to make tons of money. On the contrary, most breeders realize little profit from the litters they produce and produce them only out of love for the breed and their desire to ensure the breed's future.

BE PREPARED! Ten Questions You Should Ask the Breeder

1. How long has the kennel been in business?
2. How many litters a year are produced?
3. Are the sire and dam on the premises? (Note: Sometimes only one parent is on the premises—usually the dam—because the breeder has bred with another kennel. This is perfectly fine as long as you are provided with all the necessary information on the sire so you can feel free to contact that breeder as well.)
4. Can you provide a veterinary reference?
5. Can you provide names and phone numbers of people who have purchased your dogs?
6. What kinds of temperaments are typical of your breedings?
7. Has you ever had any genetic defects in your lines? If so, what are they and how have you corrected the problem?
8. Can you provide a health certificate with each puppy as well as first shots?
9. Are your litters AKC registered?
10. Do you provide a buyer's contract in which you will guarantee to take the dog back at any time during its life for any reason?

Finding the right breeder is, by far, the best way to ensure that you will get the Russell that you want. It's also a good idea to shop around for a local breeder. That way, you can visit the kennel and see the puppies as well as the sire and the dam in person, rather than having to rely on photos sent from a distance.

Helpful Hints

There are several ways to locate a breeder:

- Call your local dog club.
- Check the newspaper classifieds.
- Contact the PRTAA at *www.prtaa.org.*
- Go to dog shows.
- Contact the AKC.
- Call the local humane society.
- Ask doggy friends.

Probably the most fun way to meet Russell breeders is to attend a dog show. You can attend a specialty show at which only Russell's will be exhibited, an all-breed show, or agility and obedience trials. You can log on to *www.infodog.com* to access a complete monthly list of shows all over the United States. If you go to an AKC-sanctioned all-breed conformation show, find out ahead of time when Russell's are scheduled for judging. Attending shows will give you an opportunity to meet and talk to a variety of Russell breeders as well as to owners who are showing their dogs. In general, it is an invaluable educational experience for the prospective dog owner as well as a great place to meet other Russell enthusiasts who will be very forthright and honest about the breed. Most Russell

BE PREPARED! Ten Questions the Breeder Should Ask You

1. Are you a first-time Russell owner?
2. Why do you want a Russell, and what qualities are you looking for?
3. Do you have children, and if so, what are their ages?
4. Where will your dog be kept?
5. Do you live in a private house or an apartment or condo?
6. If in a house, do you have a fenced yard? If in an apartment or condo, do you have access to a dog park or similar facility?
7. Describe your personality: Are you energetic or laid-back, an outdoor enthusiast or a couch potato? Do you enjoy playing with dogs or just sitting and petting them?
8. Are you easily frustrated or do you stick with a task until you're successfully completed it?
9. Do you intend to enroll your Russell in an obedience class?
10. Have you ever given up a pet for any reason, and if so, why?

owners and breeders love to talk about their dogs!

After you've contacted several breeders and narrowed down your list, schedule a visit to each breeder's kennel. Reputable breeders will welcome this; some even insist upon it because they want to be assured that their puppies are going to the best homes possible. If a breeder is unwilling to allow you to visit his or her kennel, cross this breeder off your list—he or she could be hiding something.

CAUTION

Beware of a breeder who is ready to sell you a Russell without determining your suitability to own the dog. This type of a person might be interested only in money, and that means that his or her dogs could have been bred without regard to their health or safety.

When you arrive at the breeder's kennel, be prepared to ask a lot of questions and be asked just as many in return.

The purpose of asking each other pertinent questions is not only to find out important information but also to determine if you and the breeder have a rapport. It is crucial to feel both comfortable with and confident in the breeder you choose, because your breeder will be a constant source of information about your Russell as well as a support system throughout the life of your pet. Like proud grandparents, most breeders take pleasure in following the lives of their puppies as they go out into the world of their new families.

Before you buy your Russell, make sure his parents have Orthopedic Foundation for Animals (OFA) and Canine Eye Registration Foundation

BE PREPARED! **The Contract**

A clearly defined, signed contract is the best way to protect both the buyer and the breeder. Most contracts will state that you need to have your puppy checked by a veterinarian within a specified time frame. Additionally, make sure that any verbal agreement you make with the breeder is also provided for in the contract.

(CERF) certificates. The puppy should also have a Brainstem Auditory Evoked Response (BAER) certificate to ensure normal hearing.

After visiting several kennels and speaking to breeders, you will be able to narrow down your choices and come up with a good match. However, once you've selected a breeder, you will probably have to wait for a puppy. As mentioned, reputable breeders have a limited number of litters per year, and generally take reservations for future litters. So be patient. Think of it as the "pregnancy" period. As you await the birth and weaning of your puppy, use the time to learn more about the breed and prepare for your puppy's arrival.

Don't be embarrassed or timid about asking a breeder for references. In most cases, breeders are so proud of their dogs that they offer references without being asked and encourage a prospective owner to talk to clients who have their dogs. Selecting the right dog is a serious business, and you need to be armed with all the information possible to make the best choice.

The Parson Russell Terrier Puppy

The first time you see a litter of Russell pups, you will smile with delight and invariably, your heart will skip a beat—they are that irresistible. In fact, you will be hard pressed to refrain from taking one or more home with you immediately. So take a deep breath, step back a few paces, and get ready to observe the pups in action while trying to be as objective as possible. Watching puppies interact with their littermates can provide quite a bit of information about each dog's personality. Does one puppy appear to be more aggressive and dominant than the others in play?

As you observe the puppies at play, one in particular will probably catch your eye. At this point, you should ask the breeder to let you see that puppy away from the others. Watch how the puppy reacts. Is he frightened or shy? Does he ignore you and amuse himself? Does he come over to you and play? Or does he grab a toy and attack it aggressively? All of these things are indicators of the puppy's temperament. As you observe the litter, you notice that no two pups are alike. The breeder can help to interpret the behavior of the puppies and, based on the qualities you are looking for, help you identify the pup that best exemplifies your criteria.

CHECKLIST

Puppy Papers

Once you've decided on a puppy, make sure the breeder supplies you with the following:

✔ A registration certificate, properly executed, that gives the date of birth, and the AKC, UKC, or CKC registration numbers of the sire and the dam

✔ A written, three-generation pedigree

✔ An inoculation record signed by the breeder's veterinarian

✔ A health record, signed by the breeder's veterinarian

✔ Basic diet and puppy care instructions

✔ A schedule for future puppy inoculations

✔ A buyer's contract

Evaluating the Puppy's Temperament

The way a puppy interacts with you can tell you a lot about his temperament. If he is content to be held and licks your face and nose, he's definitely going to be a people dog and very attached to his owner. On the other hand, if, when you pick him up, he wiggles to get away from you and back to his littermates, he'll probably grow into a more independent sort. Try turning the puppy on his back. Does he put up a real struggle? If so, he has a strong, dominant streak. Does the puppy look at you when you talk to him or follow your movements? This is the mark of a highly intelligent pup. Observing

If the new puppy will be coming into a family situation, try to have all or as many of the family members as possible present during the selection process. This will allow you to observe the chemistry between the puppy and other family members.

how the puppies respond will help you make a selection based on your needs.

When assessing a litter of puppies, it's a good idea to look for a dog who is both friendly and outgoing, without being overly aggressive in play. Usually, this will be the most even-tempered pup in the bunch. Often the biggest puppy in the litter because of his size will become the dominant one. So, too, the runt of the litter, may grow into either a timid dog or one with a Napoleon complex!

Choosing an Adult Parson Russell Terrier

Although puppies are adorable, they are also a lot of work, especially in the first few months. If your lifestyle and daily schedule don't permit you to dedicate the time needed to rear a puppy, you should probably consider getting an adult dog. Breeders sometimes have adult dogs for sale. Often these are dogs they don't intend to use in their breeding program. This is a unique opportunity for a buyer to get a very fine-quality, well-trained dog that the breeder simply wants to place in a good pet home. This could be an ideal match for the prospective owner who really wants a Russell but for one reason or another can't take a puppy. An adult Russell is also a good choice for a home with children. Another advantage of an adult dog is that what you see is what you get. Puppies are developing until they are 18 months old, so you never really know with absolute certainty how he will turn out, based on what he looks like at 8 weeks of age.

Choosing a Rescue Parson Russell Terrier

Rescue dogs often get a bad rap. This is especially true of the Russell. One assumes that they end up in shelters because they are bad dogs. This is hardly ever the case. Usually they end up there because they had bad or irresponsible owners who neglected to do their homework about the breed before bringing the dog home, and thus were either ill equipped or unwilling to commit to the challenges of owning a Russell. That said, most Russells who find themselves in shelters are there simply because they exhibited typical Russell behavior. For this reason, the prospective Russell owner needs to understand completely what he is getting into before, not after, he buys the dog. This will save heartbreak on both sides.

However, if you are 100 percent confident in your heart and soul that the Parson Russell Terrier is the canine life companion that will best complement and enrich you, consider adopting one from a rescue organization. This is an especially viable alternative if you are more interested in an adult dog than a puppy. You will also have the added satisfaction of giving a second chance to a dog whose only "crime" was being a Russell. If you think you might be interested in a rescue dog, check out Russell Rescue (*www.Russellrescue.com*).

What Is Russell Rescue?

Russell Rescue is dedicated to finding new homes for Parson Russell Terriers that have either been recovered from shelters and pounds, or turned in by families who could no longer care for them because of a change in circumstances or, more often, because theirs was the wrong type of environment for a Russell to begin with. Because of the growing popularity of the breed, many more people are buying Russells based on dogs they see on television or in the movies. As a result, they are often unprepared to deal with the reality of the breed, and consequently, the problem of unwanted dogs is growing.

The goal of Russell Rescue is to recover misplaced and unwanted Parson Russell Terriers and place them into proper homes before they are euthanized in shelters.

Rescue Russells come in all shapes, sizes, and personalities. When they enter the rescue program, they are carefully evaluated for any physical, behavioral, and health problems. After any problems are accessed and addressed, the dog is available for adoption. Be prepared to fill out a detailed adoption form. Russell Rescue takes great pains to match the right dog to the right owner to ensure a successful adoption.

Evaluating the Puppy's Health

The most heartbreaking thing for any new owner is to find out that his new dog is not as healthy as he was led to believe. Although any reputable breeder will take back a puppy that is found to have a health problem, usually the new owner has grown so attached to the pup that he can't bear to give it up. Thus, before you select your boy, don't be afraid to examine him carefully.

- **Ears:** Look at the inside of his ears. They should be pink, smooth, and clear without any lumps, bumps, swelling, rashes, or sign of wax buildup or ear mites. Sniff his ear canal. It should smell sweet without any putrid odor.
- **Eyes:** They should be clear and bright, with pupils the same size. There should be no excessive discharge.
- **Nose:** It should be moist and cool to the touch; if it's hot or dry, he could be running a fever.
- **Mouth and Teeth:** The teeth should be white and clean, the gums pink, and his breath fresh.
- **Legs and Body:** Feel the legs and body for any sign of lumps or other swelling.
- **Feet and Nails:** Check his foot pads for any cuts, cracks, or foreign objects. Check between the toes for sores or ticks.
- **Skin and Coat:** The skin should be smooth and clean with a healthy gloss on the coat. He should be free of dandruff, rashes, scabs, or other lesions.
- **Tail:** The tail should be free of any bumps.

Your puppy's temperature should be between 100°F and 102.5°F. Use a rectal thermometer to get a reading.

CHECKLIST

Is a Parson Russell Terrier the Right Dog for You?

✔ Are you aware of the unique needs and character of a working terrier? (Many dog owners are overwhelmed by the demands of a Russell.)

✔ Are you aware that the Russell is first and foremost a hunting dog? (Traits and skills like digging, barking, and aggressiveness that make him an excellent hunting dog are often interpreted as bad habits that cause people to give them up.)

✔ Are you aware that a Russell needs to have an outlet for his natural instincts and energy, and lacking that, he will invent new things to do that can include destroying property, chasing cars, hunting birds or other small animals, and digging up the backyard?

✔ Are you aware that a Russell has the same or more exercise needs as a much larger dog?

✔ Are you aware that same-sex aggression and aggression toward other breeds (even breeds three times his size) of dogs is well documented in this breed?

✔ Are you aware that it is advisable that no more than two Russells of the opposite sex should ever be allowed to stay together unattended?

✔ Are you aware that the Russell is not a nonshedding breed?

✔ Are you aware that a Russell requires firm and consistent discipline?

✔ Are you aware that a Russell is extremely intelligent and will test his owner's limits throughout his life?

✔ Are you aware that a Russell will attempt to "train" his owner through a display of aggressive behavior?

✔ Are you aware that the assertive behavior of the Russell must be understood and handled properly?

✔ Are you aware that a Russell remains active well into his teen years?

✔ Are you aware that a Russell will require obedience training? (Even a well-trained dog will be tempted to chase something that catches his interest, or even disappear into a hole while you are not looking.)

✔ Are you aware that a Russell should always be leash-walked?

✔ Are you aware that a Russell needs a secure, professionally installed fenced yard?

✔ Are you aware that the Russell is, at heart, a country dog? (When made to live in a city or suburban-type environment, his needs and instincts remain the same and your lifestyle must be adjusted to meet them.)

✔ Are you aware that most behavioral problems are caused by a lack of companionship, discipline, activity, and exercise?

✔ Are you aware that a Russell will not tolerate even unintended mistreatment from a child, such as ear and tail tugging?

✔ Are you aware that a Russell is not recommended for households with children under the age of six unless you are previously experienced with this feisty turbo dog?

If you answered a resounding "yes" to *all* of the above, then congratulations: You are ready for a Russell and one of the most exhilarating experiences of a lifetime!

Chapter Four

Caring for a Parson Russell Terrier Puppy

The day you pick up your Russell puppy will be filled with excitement and anticipation. Once you bring the puppy home, be prepared for even more excitement as he becomes acclimated into a new family environment. If there are children in the house, make sure they understand that the new puppy is not a toy, and should not be pulled, handled roughly, or passed from child to child. Most important, you should bring your puppy into a tranquil environment to make his transition less traumatic. Remember, this is the first time he will be separated from his mother and his littermates, so you want him to feel reassured that he has come to a safe and loving place.

Furthermore, if there are children in the household, lay down some ground rules before the puppy arrives. These should include

1. making children aware that they must pick up all their toys so that the puppy doesn't get into them;
2. teaching children to exhibit good manners and respect for the puppy;
3. agreeing on the exact words and phrases you will all use to correct unwanted behavior in the puppy; and
4. designating who will clean up after the puppy.

If there are several children in the household, each may be given a specific job in the care of the puppy. This will not only teach children responsibility but will also allow them to bond with the new member of the family. Children should also be strongly advised never to hit or yell at the puppy.

After establishing the puppy house rules with the rest of the family, you'll need to prepare for his arrival. This will make your first days together happy and free of stress. A young

CAUTION

Do not allow small children to carry the puppy. Puppies are very wriggly and can easily be dropped or cause a small child to fall. If the child wants to hold the puppy, first ask the child to sit and then place the puppy in the child's arms. Never allow small children to be alone and unsupervised with the puppy.

puppy is curious about everything in his environment, and will delight in exploring. The puppy uses his mouth to sample anything he finds interesting. He cannot distinguish between benign and harmful objects, so you will have to do that for him before his arrival. Get started by going through your house, particularly the area where the puppy will be initially confined, and be sure the area is "puppy-proof."

Puppy-Proofing Your Home

- Remove all objects from the floor that are not specifically designated as puppy toys.
- Remove plants and bric-a-brac from tables and stands.
- Remove electrical cords from any area the puppy will have access to.
- Cover exposed electric sockets with plastic socket covers.
- Tack down any dangling cords from televisions, air conditioners, and other electronic equipment, as well as from window treatments.
- Section off stairs from your puppy with a tension or other puppy gate.
- Install "child-proof" locks on drawers and cabinets, particularly in the kitchen area.
- Section off a portion of a room, usually the kitchen, as the "puppy area" until your new boy is house-trained and thoroughly acclimated to his new environment.
- Close off all outdoor decks, balconies, and stairwells.
- If you have sliding glass doors, place several decals on the door at the puppy's eye level, so he will not mistake it for an open space.
- Lock away all household cleaning products, toxic substances, insecticides, medicines, over-the-counter remedies, and alcoholic beverages in a high cabinet, away from the puppy's reach.
- Ditto for food, snacks, and candies, especially chocolate.

CAUTION

Some common household and outdoor plants are highly toxic to your Russell: milkweed, oleander, azaleas, mistletoe, English holly berries, philodendron, rhododendron, water hemlock, and foxglove, among others. Ask your local nursery for a complete list of plants that can be poisonous to animals. In addition to all household cleaners and insecticides, also keep antifreeze, paint thinner, rodent traps, insect baits, air fresheners, and toilet cleaners locked away.

Never underestimate your Russell puppy's ability to find forbidden objects. The best preventive is to remove the temptation and thereby avert a potentially serious, if not deadly, situation.

Keep the lid of your toilet closed at *all* times. This is an important safety measure. Many a thirsty dog has wandered into a bathroom for a drink out

SHOPPING LIST

Puppy Needs

There are several things you'll need to purchase before bringing your Russell into his new home. Having these puppy supplies available will make life much easier for you and your new Russell. There are many pet catalogs available online that make shopping convenient and stress free. However, if you prefer to have the experience of shopping in person for your puppy, any of the major pet supply stores will have what you need.

✔ **Dog Crate:** Most breeders will suggest that you crate-train your Russell. The crate functions in several ways: as a "den" where the puppy can be quiet and undisturbed; as a housetraining tool; as a time-out place when the puppy gets overstimulated; and as a safe retreat when you have to leave the puppy home alone for short periods of time.

✔ **Puppy Pen:** Puppies can be very active, and a good way to let your Russell expend some of his considerable energy is to set up a puppy exercise pen where he can have fun in a confined, supervised area. This way you can keep an eye on him and he'll keep out of trouble.

✔ **Leash and Collar:** A good leather or nylon leash of four to six feet is the best choice. Both are very durable. Chain leashes can snap, and they can also be very noisy. A leather or nylon collar is also a good choice. Remember, a puppy will grow out of a collar fairly quickly, so buy one with several notches, so you won't have to keep replacing it. You should also purchase a choke collar, which should be used only when walking the puppy and when

you start obedience training. Never leave a choke collar on a dog for any other reason.

✔ **Harness:** Some owners prefer to walk their dogs using a harness rather than a choke collar. This is fine, as long as you make sure the harness fits perfectly and is slip-proof. It's best to take your dog to the pet store and have a salesperson help you find the right fit.

✔ **ID Tag:** Most pet stores can make an identification tag for your dog while you wait. Alternately, you can buy one from a pet catalog after filling out the pertinent information. Delivery usually takes between one and two weeks. You should have your pet's ID tag already attached to his collar when you pick him up from the breeder.

✔ **Feeding Bowls:** Bowls come in a variety of sizes and textures, from stainless steel to vinyl to the fancier ceramic types. You'll need one bowl for the puppy's food and another for his water.

✔ **Bedding:** The puppy should have his own bed. Again, there are many choices, many shapes and sizes, but all that's really necessary is a comfortable place where the puppy can curl up and sleep.

✔ **Toys:** Most owners go overboard when it comes to buying toys for their puppy. However, all toys are not created equal. If you buy vinyl toys, make sure they are sturdy and too big for the puppy to swallow. The best choices are Nylabones, which come in different flavors. Not only are they a great teething toy, but they are virtually indestructible and will provide your Russell with many hours of satisfying and safe fun.

of the toilet only to be poisoned to death by the cleaning agents in the bowl! Get in the habit of keeping the bathroom door closed, even as your puppy grows into adulthood. The normal bathroom contains far too many substances that can be deadly to pets.

It's also important to safety-check the outside of your home. The yard should be enclosed by a fence five feet or higher. The fencing should extend below the surface of the ground to keep the Russell from digging under it. If your fence is already in place, then consider adding a strong mesh or similar barrier that's at least six to eight inches deep along the perimeter of the fence. Check your fence for any holes, breaks or weak spots and have them repaired immediately by a professional. Make certain that there are no sharp objects like broken glass, knives, or hunting or fishing equipment lying around.

If you're a golfer, lock away those bags of golf balls. They are small enough for a Russell to swallow! Instead, give him a new tennis ball to play with.

Puppy's First Day

If you've prepared properly for your Russell's arrival, you'll be better able to enjoy your first day together. Before bringing him inside the house, take him to a spot in the yard where you want him to relieve himself. Puppies need to go out often, so he will probably comply. Once inside, the puppy will be curious and excited, and will want to explore his new environment, but don't give him the run of the place. Introduce him to the house one room at a time, and make sure he is not left anywhere unsupervised.

Even though puppies have lots of energy, they also tire easily and need to take frequent naps. Once the puppy has had a little playtime with the rest of the family, bring him to the area you've sectioned off and let him settle in for a snooze. Don't wake him when he's sleeping, as he needs his rest. When he does awaken, he'll have to relieve himself. The puppy will probably sleep through the night. But don't be surprised if he whines and cries when you leave him alone in his bed. He is used to sleeping with his littermates, so he will naturally be lonely and frightened.

Crate-Training

Giving your Russell puppy his own special place is one of the most important steps in the training process. Crate-training him is an extremely effective way to help him feel safe and confident. This is especially true for the
high-energy Russell, who can benefit enormously from having his own den
where he can wind down, chill out, and generally keep out of mischief.
Many breeders will begin crate-training a puppy before he goes to his new
home. It's important to keep in mind that although a crate looks like the
equivalent of "doggy jail," it's quite the opposite. The puppy should learn to
associate his crate with pleasurable "alone" time where he can lie back and
retreat from the world around him. Many dogs will go into their crates without being asked just to have their own private space. Thus, you should
never use the crate as punishment. You should make it as comfortable a

FYI: Crate Choices

There are several types of crates you can purchase, but whichever you decide on, make sure it is neither too big nor too small. A proper-size crate is one that allows the dog to stand at full height, turn around, and lie down comfortably. Make the crate as comfortable as possible by adding a nice mat and some toys so your puppy will enjoy his time there. He should also have fresh water available through a water feeder, which can be purchased separately and snapped onto the inside of the crate. Some crates come with their own water and food dishes. Never leave your Russell in a crate for long hours on end.

refuge as possible by adding a cozy mat where the puppy can curl up. Put some of his toys there as well. That way, when he wakes up, he can amuse himself. As your Russell matures, you may want to keep the crate accessible to him by leaving the door open so that any time he feels the need, he can go inside to be by himself. You'll be surprised at how often your dog will seek the privacy of his crate.

Helpful Hints

If you want to train your puppy to sleep in his crate, keep the crate next to your bed so that you can hear him cry when he has to go out. Otherwise, he will be forced to relieve himself in his sleeping quarters. Don't buy a crate that is too big or your Russell will use one corner of it as a bathroom!

Allowing your Russell the opportunity to retreat to his crate can be very helpful if you have younger children in the house. Children will naturally want to run and play with the new addition to the family, but the puppy will need his own place to "get away" from all that super-charged activity, and a crate fits the bill very nicely. Children should be told that the puppy's crate is off limits, and that way, they will learn to respect the puppy's space and his need to wind down and catch a nap.

If the breeder has not introduced your puppy to the crate, then introduce him gradually as soon as you bring him home. Play with him for a few minutes, then take him out to relieve himself, then put him in his crate for a short time. He may cry at first, but if you put some of his toys in with him, he'll soon settle down. You can gradually increase his time in the crate until he begins to view it as his private den. As the puppy gets acclimated to being in his crate, you may be tempted to leave him there for long periods of time. Don't do that unless you have to be out of the house for a few hours. Leaving a puppy in a crate for long periods of time day in and day out will not only impede his socialization process, but will result

If your Russell has an accident in the house, do not ever rub his nose in his excrement or hit him with a newspaper. This will instill fear in your pet. Elimination is a natural process for a dog, and if he's punished for doing so, it will confuse him and may lead to aggressive behavior. It's up to you to train him to relieve himself in a designated area. As stated, your Russell should never be punished for having an accident.

in a very frustrated animal. Keep in mind that although the crate is a great training tool, it is not meant to be a prison. Use it judiciously and with common sense.

Housetraining

Besides functioning as your puppy's retreat, the crate is very useful in the housetraining process. Newborn puppies are unable to urinate on their own, so their mother licks them to stimulate elimination. As their systems mature, and the puppy is able to crawl, he will instinctively move away from the place where he and his littermates sleep to relieve himself. Thus, when you place your Russell in his crate, which he looks on as his den, he instinctively will try not to eliminate there. Keep in mind that a puppy will have to relieve himself every couple of hours, so be vigilant, and when it looks like he has to go, take him out of the crate and outside to the spot where you want him to eliminate.

A puppy will have to go out often, so it's important to be able to recognize what his body language is telling you. If he starts making circles, sniffing, and whining, that's his signal that he has to eliminate. Scoop him up right away and take him outside to the place you've designated as his "relief station" during the housetraining process. Once he eliminates outside, praise him effusively and give him a treat. This will teach him to associate relieving himself outdoors with positive things. Repeat this procedure each time you take your Russell out. You'll be surprised at how quickly he'll catch on.

Associating a word or phrase with the puppy's act of relieving himself can be very effective later on. For example, when you bring your Russell to his relief station, you might say the words "Make potty" or whatever words or catchphrase you want to associate with the act. As the Russell matures, you can use the same words as "cues" to communicate with him.

Helpful Hints

Some puppies respond to housetraining more quickly than others. But don't expect your Russell to get his bathroom etiquette down overnight. Give the puppy several months to fully adjust, and above all, be consistent in your housetraining methods; otherwise, he'll get confused. However, if your puppy continues to have frequent accidents, there may be a physical reason and you should consult with your veterinarian.

By the time your Russell is 12 weeks old, he should be able to sleep through the night without your having to get up and take him out. But accidents will happen no matter how vigilant you are. Even as the puppy matures into adulthood, he'll have an occasional accident. The culprit can be anything from an upset stomach to a urinary tract infection to not being taken out for too many hours. The important thing is that you should never reprimand your Russell for having an accident. A dog does not want to soil his living quarters and will usually resort to doing so only if he can't help it.

Make it a general practice to take your Russell out right after he eats, after he wakes up from a nap, after exercise or playtime, and before you go to bed. This will help with the housetraining process because it will get your puppy used to a regular schedule.

Helpful Hints

To reinforce boundaries, you may want to spray furniture legs with a nontoxic "doggy-no" product like bitter apple spray. However, never spray the product directly into your puppy's mouth!

Establishing Boundaries

A puppy needs to have boundaries and needs to know from day one who is in charge. This will make his life and yours happy and tranquil. If you don't establish boundaries, you will plant the seed for behavioral issues later on.

First and foremost, the Russell puppy must know that you, are the leader, not him, and that he must learn to respect your authority. He must also learn which behavior is acceptable and which is not. All of this can and should be accomplished in a positive, nonthreatening manner.

Start by setting physical boundaries for your Russell. He should not be allowed the run of the house, but should be confined in a sectioned-off "safe zone" while you go about your daily chores. It's fine for him to explore other parts of the house, but only when you are there to supervise him.

Next, set behavioral boundaries for your puppy. It's normal for a puppy to use his mouth in play. He doesn't distinguish between your hands, your designer shoes, or your furniture. It's up to you to show him what he is allowed to pick up or chew. You can accomplish this by redirecting his mouth from your arm or shoe to one of his toys. When the puppy takes the toy, praise him. Be consistent and he'll soon get the message and understand his limits. Similarly, if you don't want your puppy jumping on the sofa or on your bed, redirect his actions. When he jumps on the sofa, pick him up and carry him over to his bed or approved puppy spot, gently push him into a sitting position, and praise him.

Breed Needs

Early handling as well as events that occur during the first two to four months of your Russell's life is absolutely critical in his social development. If puppies are not exposed to stimuli such as other people, animals, and new environments during this period, they may become fearful, leading to either timidity or aggression as the puppy matures. This is particularly important in the case of a Russell puppy. He was originally bred to be a working hunter, and that instinct remains strong. Therefore, expect to put more effort into socializing him. The more he is exposed to people and other animals, the better he will adapt to life as a pet and companion member of a household.

The N-Word

You should teach your puppy the *no* command immediately. Anytime he exhibits forbidden behavior, simply tell him *"No."* There's no need to raise your voice and frighten him. If he jumps on the sofa, just use a firm tone in your normal voice: *"No, Jack."* Immediately take him off the sofa and bring him to his mat or bed, then pet and praise him: "Good boy!"

This will not only teach your Russell boundaries, but will also impress upon him that obeying is quite pleasant. As with all training, consistency is the key. Your Russell will continue to learn boundaries throughout his life, and the goal is to make it a positive and pleasant experience.

As your Russell grows, he will be far more secure and far better able to encounter new things without fear if he understands what his place is and what his limits are.

ACTIVITIES **The Social Scene**

As soon as you bring your Russell puppy home, you can begin socializing him by gradually introducing him to new situations:

- Enroll him puppy in puppy kindergarten—this will give him an opportunity to play with other puppies.
- Leash-walk him in your neighborhood.
- Bring him to a dog park, but always keep him leashed.
- Allow strangers to pet him, after asking your permission.
- Attend a dog show with him, after he has all his vaccinations.
- When he's old enough, enroll him in obedience class.
- Ask a stranger to give your puppy a treat—this will teach him to look forward to meeting people and discourage hand-shyness.
- Take him to outdoor restaurants where pets are allowed.

Socialization

To become a well-adjusted member of society, your puppy has to be socialized. He must become comfortable with other people and with the world at large. The puppy's initial socialization process actually begins in the litter, interacting with his mother and littermates. Breeders make it a point to handle each puppy in the early weeks of life. This is to ensure that the puppies will adapt more easily to their new homes once they leave the kennel. In the puppy's first three months of development, he should be introduced to as many new people and situations as possible.

The more opportunities you give your Russell to meet new people in new environments, the more well balanced and self-confident he will become. Remember, a Russell that has not been properly socialized will become timid and fearful, which in turn can lead to aggressive tendencies later on.

Breed Truths

The primary socialization period for your Russell begins at 3 weeks of age and starts to diminish by the time he's 12 weeks old. After that, he may start to regress and exhibit fearfulness toward new people, animals, or situations. This can be avoided by continuing his social interactions as he grows and develops. However, make sure your puppy has had all of his shots before you begin introducing him to other animals so he will not be exposed to infection.

Puppy Health

Puppies have a natural immunity from diseases when they are born. This is passed to them from their dam, provided she has been properly immunized, but it lasts for only a few weeks. When you bring your Russell puppy home, he should come with a health certificate from the breeder's veterinarian attesting to his good health. He also should have received his first set of puppy shots. Make an appointment with your own veterinarian as soon as possible. It's a good idea to introduce your Russell to the veterinarian when he's in good health. That way, the puppy's first visit will be a positive one and he won't be fearful when he has to return to the veterinarian for the rest of his shots or other health issues.

Choosing a Veterinarian

The relationship between you and your veterinarian is a special one. If you don't have a veterinarian, do some research before

FYI: Puppy Vaccination Chart

6–8 weeks	canine distemper, infectious hepatitis, parainfluenza, canine adenovirus type 2, coronavirus, parvovirus; re-vaccination every 2–3 weeks until 16 weeks
12 weeks	leptospirosis, and Lyme disease (if recommended)
14–16 weeks	rabies (some veterinarians prefer to wait until the puppy is 1 year old to give the first rabies shot)
At One Year	boosters for most vaccines; then every three years for core vaccines

deciding which one will be the best choice for you and your Russell. Not all veterinarians are created equal. Some have a bias against breeds that they deem "difficult." Ask if the veterinarian has other Russells in his practice and his thoughts on the breed. If you hear a lot of negatives, cross that veterinarian off your list and find another one. There is sometimes a tendency to go with an older, more experienced veterinarian. But many times, a younger veterinarian will be more accessible, and more forthcoming during consultations, and will encourage you to call if you have questions. This can give a first-time dog owner, especially, an added sense of security. It's really about you and your veterinarian being on the same wavelength. So pick a veterinarian with whom you feel both comfortable and confident.

Russell Puppy Problems and Solutions

Puppies are wonderful, entertaining creatures, but they also have a penchant for getting into mischief more often than not. This is especially true of the Russell, who will invent ways to boggle your mind and try your patience, almost from day one. It will be apparent right away that your new puppy has a mind of his own, and despite the Russell's intelligence, his willfulness makes him more difficult to train than most breeds. That's why it is imperative that you address any behavioral problem that arises immediately and not dismiss it simply as "cute" puppy behavior. If you give your Russell pup the upper

Helpful Hints

A determined Russell will dig under most fences within an hour or less, despite training. Try to head off this problem by taking your puppy to "Go To Earth" classes, where dogs are taught to channel their digging instincts!

HOME BASICS
Puppy Problems

The following are some common puppy problems and solutions:

Problem	Solution
Jumping, pawing—Your puppy does this to get attention.	Don't yell at him; just turn and walk away. The next time your Russell approaches you, gently push him into a sitting position before he can jump. Then praise him for sitting.
Playing rough—If you use your hands in play, your puppy sees them as fun things to grab or bite.	Don't use your hands when you play with your Russell. Instead, play with him using a toy or a ball and teach him to fetch. Avoid games of tug-of-war, as this can lead to aggression in a Russell.
Mouthing—Puppies love to put their mouth on everything; they also love to chew, especially when they are teething.	If your Russell nips or chews at your hands or feet, say "no" firmly, take your hand or foot away from him, and offer him a Nylabone or Kong toy instead. When he accepts the bone or toy, praise him.
Aggression—Some Russell puppies are naturally more aggressive than others, especially if your puppy was the dominant one in the litter.	Your Russell puppy should be left with his dam until he is 8–12 weeks of age, the longer the better. The dam instinctively teaches the puppies not to be aggressive. However, if your puppy still exhibits aggressive tendencies, enroll him in a puppy training class as soon as he has received all his puppy shots. This will allow you to work with your Russell on obedience in a fun environment and will also help him feel comfortable with other dogs and people.

hand, he's smart enough to take it, and that will spell big trouble as he matures. This does not mean that you should be harsh or unfeeling with your puppy. Never yell at him or frighten him. Any and all corrections should be made gently and in a loving but firm manner.

CHECKLIST
Feeding Do's and Don'ts

✔ Do ask your breeder for a recommendation; unless you have a good reason to change foods, it's probably best to keep the puppy on the same food the breeder was feeding.

✔ Do feed your puppy at the same times each day—puppies need three to four small meals per day until they are 16 weeks old.

✔ Do put him on a high-quality puppy food—read the label and make sure the food is free from fillers; a good puppy food should say on the package that is it "complete and balanced for growth."

✔ Do your research—there are many commercial brands to choose from.

✔ Do check the percentages of protein, fat, and other nutrients listed on the package label; puppies need more protein than adult dogs.

✔ Don't overfeed your puppy—an overweight puppy will develop health problems.

✔ Don't feed your puppy table scraps—people food adds calories your Russell doesn't need.

✔ Don't feed him between scheduled mealtimes.

✔ Don't change his diet abruptly—if you change his food, gradually mix the new food in with the old food over a two-week period, decreasing the old food while systematically increasing the new.

Puppy Nutrition

Your Russell's nutritional needs and requirements are far greater during puppyhood than at any other time in his life. That's because his bones, joints, muscles, and internal organs are developing and growing during this period. His immune system is learning to protect him. His brain is also developing. A lot is happening in a very short time. If you consider that in his first year of life your Russell puppy will go through as many changes as a human does from birth to fourteen, it's no wonder that he has to have the right level of nutrition to support healthy growth and development.

Before bringing your Russell home, decide on the puppy food you will be feeding him and have it available. The following are the most important nutritional components:

- **Protein**—the key building block of muscle, skin, coat, organs and other tissues. During this period of growth, a puppy needs abundant protein.
- **Calcium and Phosphorus**—necessary for healthy bones and teeth. They must be present in the correct ratios so bones and teeth develop correctly.

- **Omega Fatty Acids, Including Linoleic Acid**—provides complete and balanced nutrition, promotes a healthy immune system, and helps keep your Russell puppy's skin and coat healthy.

The food you choose to feed your puppy has to supply all of these and more. How the ingredients are mixed is equally important.

Dry, Semi-Moist, or Canned?

There are many types of puppy food available.

Dry food is the most popular and a good choice because it tastes good, it's easy to store, it provides excellent balanced nutrition, and it has the added bonus of being good for your puppy's teeth.

Semi-moist food is also popular because it's easier to chew, but it will not have the benefits of keeping your puppy's teeth clean.

Canned food, although very palatable for your pup, also contains a lot of water and less nutrition per pound of food, so you will have to feed your puppy a higher volume to get the same nutritional benefits as the dry or semi-moist.

Helpful Hints

When you are shopping for puppy food, be sure to compare dry with dry and canned with canned to get an accurate nutritional comparison. A good rule of thumb is to review the nutritional claims of each food and look for one that is appropriate for your puppy's life stage. You will also want to stick with a food that your puppy enjoys, one that is readily available in pet stores, and one within your budget.

Living with a Parson Russell Terrier

nviting an animal into your life is not so different from asking another human being to share your home and hearth. Sometimes you get more than you expected; other times, you get something entirely different. In either case, all initial honeymoon periods eventually give way to reality. This is true whenever creatures occupy the same living space. Invariably, adjustments have to be made, individual differences accounted for, patience and respect accorded on each side. No matter how cute Jack may be, once he moves in, starts leaving his dirty laundry all over the house, blasts his fav rap music into the wee hours, and turns the garage into his personal gym, something's got to give. Basic ground rules must be laid down or chaos will become the order of the day.

This is equally true when Jack's canine counterpart, the irresistibly adorable Russell, checks into your home and heart. No doubt, one look from his deep brown eyes is enough to charm the socks off you, and you will completely understand why you fell head over heels for him in the first place. But be forewarned: Five minutes later, this pint-sized dynamo may be running relays around your living room with one of those socks dangling forlornly between gleefully clenched teeth, and no power on earth is going to pry it loose.

Although this type of spirited behavior is part of the Russell's allure, it can also be unsettling, especially to the first-time owner who was expecting a sweet, docile lapdog, not a relentless canine roller coaster.

Breed Truths

The Russell is a high-energy, often stubborn big dog trapped in a small dog's body. He is as playful as he is fearless and as intelligent as he is willful, and he needs positive outlets for his boundless enthusiasm. It's important to remember and appreciate that he was originally bred as a working dog to hunt and go to ground, not to be a house pet. No matter how well trained he may be, these instincts can never be totally eradicated, but they can be redirected to make him a happy and fully integrated member of his human family. To accomplish this, you must provide him with productive activities.

COMPATIBILITY Is a Russell the Best Breed for You?

	Rating
ENERGY LEVEL	● ● ● ●
EXERCISE REQUIREMENTS	● ● ● ●
PLAYFULNESS	● ● ● ●
PROTECTIVENESS	● ● ● ●
AFFECTION LEVEL	● ● ● ●
FRIENDLINESS TOWARD OTHER PETS	●
FRIENDLINESS TOWARD STRANGERS	●
FRIENDLINESS TOWARD CHILDREN	● ●
EASE OF TRAINING	● ●
GROOMING REQUIREMENTS	● ●
SHEDDING	● ●
SPACE REQUIREMENTS	● ● ● ●
OK FOR BEGINNERS	●

4 Dots = Highest rating on scale

A bored Russell is a recipe for disaster. The same instinct that makes him a superior hunter predisposes him to an active lifestyle. This is not a dog you can dress up and put on display. He is a mover and a shaker and will not suffer to become a couch potato.

The World According to the Russell

If the Russell could talk, and most Russell owners will swear to you that they do, indeed have their own special language, he would tell you that he thinks he's the king of the world, and has no intention of abdicating his throne. If you have any doubt, just watch him strut his stuff: head held high, strong, confident gait, a demeanor that says *Look at me, I'm something special*, and he is!

A Russell sees himself as bigger than a mastiff and fiercer than a lion. He can be aggressive with other dogs, regardless of their size. Consequently, he will stand his ground and never back down if confronted by a larger dog. On the contrary, many a big dog has backed away from an altercation with a Russell. This same fearlessness, however, can be a Russell's undoing.

Because the Russell sees himself as lord of the universe, it follows that he regards his home as his castle and is very particular about whom he will allow within its walls. Though people friendly, the Russell is cautious with strangers and can sometimes take an intense dislike to certain individuals,

for no apparent reason. The Russell is also exceptionally protective of his family and often favors one family member over the others. It is not unusual for a Russell to follow his favorite everywhere, even into the bathroom. Many owners amusingly refer to the Russell as their shadow. Although this can be a cute and endearing trait, it can also present a problem if you work and your Russell is left alone in the house for long hours at a time. For this reason, the Russell fares better in a household where he has human interaction throughout the day. He is a very social animal, and if left on his own for long periods of time, it could lead to separation anxiety and result in destructive behavior.

Breed Truths

Even though the Russell can look and sound ferocious, he is still no match for a big dog. Nonetheless, he will fight a more formidable opponent to the death and end up on the losing end. This trait makes the Russell his own worst enemy and as such, the owner should take care to avoid any and all confrontations with other dogs.

The Russell is fiercely loyal and devoted to his owner. So much so, that once he has bonded with you, he craves and demands your attention and companionship, and why not? You are his entire universe and he wants to be with you all the time! It doesn't matter where you are or what you are doing, your boy Jack is happiest right at your heels. You don't have to look good for him, wear the latest designer duds, or be sporting a new mani-cure—he doesn't care. His love for you is completely unconditional! Try finding that kind of devotion anywhere else! Moreover, the Russell is so observant that he has been known to mimic human behaviors in ways that will both startle and amuse you. One Russell owner reported that whenever she got down on her exercise mat to do daily stretches, her dog got on the floor next to her and rolled from side to side, stretching his legs in rhythm with her movements! How smart is that?

To make living together a pleasure rather than a challenge, it's a good idea to invent fun things to do with your Russell. When drawing up a list, keep in mind that both his energy and intelligence level are extremely high. Don't be afraid to challenge your little guy with activity that is both fun and productive.

- Establish a daily playtime when you and your Russell can kick up your heels.
- Enroll in an obedience class; it will give your Russell and you a sense of both accomplishment and teamwork.
- Give your Russell a designated task to perform, like training him to bring you the morning newspaper.

Are You Ready for a Russell?

Is there an unwritten "rollerblade clause" in the life contract between you and young Jack? If not, you are going to need one. Fanciers of the breed as well as anyone who has ever owned a Russell will tell you that life with these turbo dogs is the ultimate ride in the fast lane. It's both a challenge and chuckle a minute; it's as ferocious as it is pure fun; and at the end of the day, it's totally exasperating and completely exhilarating. Whether the scales will tip more toward the one side than the other depends largely on your perspective and expectations.

Despite his adorable appearance and that appealing twinkle in his eyes, the Russell is high maintenance and not the ideal house-mate for everyone. Interestingly, he would be the first to agree. Although they are peo-ple dogs, Russells are also very discriminat-ing about the humans with whom they choose to form lasting relationships. If you're a natural athlete and free spirit like your Russell is, count yourself lucky; then buckle up and enjoy the ride.

Fun Facts

Russells appear to be delighted with rocks, probably because they love anything that requires digging. Russells love to dig up rocks, then bury them again, then dig them out and bury them all over again, and continue this for hours on end. If your boy becomes fascinated with rocks, be vigilant and don't allow him to chew them, as they may crack or wear down his teeth.

The Russell Personality

All Russells have strong personalities and exhibit equally strong likes and dislikes. It's important to remember that the natural instinct of the Russell is to chase and to hunt since he was bred as a working dog used to track rodents and other small prey. The Russell is also very intelligent, and for that reason he can be difficult to train simply

BE PREPARED! Russell Pros and Cons

PROS

- **small size**—This is great if you live in a condo or apartment, or just prefer a small breed.
- **athletic**—If you wake up each morning, slip into your running shoes, and prepare to clock a few miles around the local park, he's the perfect running mate.
- **alert**—A throwback to his hunting genes, he is ever vigilant and makes a great watchdog.
- **energetic**—If you have a lot of energy, then you'll feel right at home with this little guy, because he's always itching for something to do.
- **sociable**—He is definitely a "people" dog, but one who chooses his "friends" wisely.
- **intelligent**—He is also very smart and is a good problem solver.
- **loyal**—Once bonded to his human family, he is fiercely loyal and protective of them.

CONS

- **aggressive**—This little guy can be very aggressive, especially toward other dogs.
- **stubborn**—He wants to be the boss and tends to be very willful.
- **possessive**—He is possessive of toys and food, and in some cases, of his owner, which can lead to possessive aggression.
- **extreme exercise requirement**—Like a sporting dog, he needs to be exercised daily, almost to the point of exhaustion, to be happy.
- **digging**—he was bred to go to ground, and this instinct is firmly embedded in his DNA; if you have a flower garden, either make it off limits, or be prepared to find your plants uprooted and huge holes remaining.
- **chasing**—He was bred to hunt, and will chase just about anything that moves, including the neighbor's cat, squirrels, and cars.
- **barking**—Part of his terrier instinct is to "sound the alarm" at any and every new sight or sound.
- **shedding**—Both the smooth and broken-coated variations shed.

because he can be unpredictable. He has a mind of his own, complete with a unique ability to problem-solve. If there is an obstacle in the Russell's way, you can be sure he will figure out a way around it to get what he wants. A tempting piece of meat left on a kitchen counter is a *piece of cake* to this little Houdini, who will leap high enough to snag the treat and walk away licking his chops, with no one the wiser.

The Russell with Children

The Russell is a rugged and tough little dog who can make an excellent companion and playmate for a child. By far, the best dynamic is between a Russell and a respectful older child who can provide the high-energy, buddy relationship the dog most enjoys; the two can become great pals for life.

This is not usually true with younger children, particularly newborns and toddlers. A Russell may resent a new baby in the house. To him, it's like introducing an interloper into his established home pack.

The Russell is a proud dog and will not tolerate abuse, like tail tugging or ear and whisker pulling at the hands of a child, and will often respond in kind. For this

Helpful Hints

Make your Russell's crate off limits for kids. This way, your dog will have a place to retreat if he feels the need!

BE PREPARED! Russell Personality Profile

Intelligent	The Russell had to be highly intelligent to perform the tasks for which he was originally bred. He had to have a quick, cunning mind to trap his prey and "outfox" the fox. Although most Russells today live as house pets, their innate intelligence allows them to make accommodations according to their surroundings.
Stubborn	The Russells high level of intelligence has one big drawback: It tends to make him more stubborn than most breeds because he's already decided what he wants to do and how to accomplish it.
Aggressive	The Russell is fearless and has an unrelenting sense of purpose that predisposes him toward aggressive behavior. If he were otherwise, he never could have performed the work for which he was bred. Imagine digging as many as 15 feet or more into the ground to corner a snapping fox, and remaining there until the hunter pulls you out. Not a job for a weakling, to be sure.
Energetic	The Russell is a high-energy dog, bred as a working hunter who could spend days, not hours, digging tunnels to corner prey. It's not surprising that he can appear tireless, even after vigorous exercise, and for that reason needs positive outlets for his boundless vigor.
Loyal	One of the most winning traits of the Russell is his utter loyalty to his human family. This, too, is a throwback to his roots, where a bond of trust was formed between the human hunter and his dog. A Russell will often take some time to warm up to you, but once he chooses you as his lifelong companion, an irrevocable bond of absolute trust and loyalty is formed.
Protective	The Russell is so fearless and loyal that he will put his life on the line to protect and defend his people from all and any harm. His senses are so highly developed that he is quick to alert his owner when he perceives a threatening situation.
Life of the party	The Russell loves to have fun and will amuse you for hours with his zany antics and utter charm. He also seems to appreciate it when his human family reacts with laughter and praise for his performance!

reason, toddlers and young children under the age of seven are not generally a good match for him. Further, it's not fair to expose the Russell or any animal to this type of harassment. Usually the animal is punished or worse, when it was the child who initiated the offense. Of course, there is always the case of a Russell who adores a young child under any and all circumstances, and endures whatever the child doles out. But that's the exception rather than the rule.

An animal cannot always differentiate between mean-spiritedness and exuberance, so always supervise play between children and your Russell. Teach your child canine good manners, which include the following:

- Leave the Russell alone when he is eating or sleeping.
- Never strike or molest him physically.
- Never yell at him or chase him.

Children must be taught that the Russell is a living, breathing creature, not a stuffed toy to be tossed around at will.

Fun Facts

One of the most difficult "tricks" to teach the Russell is to sit perfectly still!

The Russell with Other Dogs

The Russell was bred to work in a pack, but because of his dominant nature, it is not uncommon for him to be aggressive toward other dogs, regardless of their size. However, if you socialize your Russell from puppyhood and raise him with another dog, this may not be a problem. Nonetheless, you can still expect your Russell to go into a *red alert* if a strange dog wanders into or near his space, such as the backyard fence. In your Russell's mind, he is merely doing his job—protecting and defending his home turf.

Russells can also be dog aggressive while out on a walk. Proper training, establishing yourself as the pack leader, and always keeping him on a leash will make walking with your Russell a pleasure rather than a battleground.

A Russell also likes being the only dog in the family pack. If another dog is introduced, the best match is often a Russell of the opposite sex. You should not introduce a smaller dog, especially a toy breed, into the household.

Breed Truths

The Russell's protective nature can be a double-edged sword if he becomes so possessive that he regards the owner as personal property. This leads to aggressive protective behavior, which if not corrected immediately, can make for an intolerable living situation.

Aggressive behavior is not only directed toward other dogs, but can also be directed at inanimate objects. For example, a Russell can take a dislike to a vacuum cleaner, a broom, or the leg of a chair and attack the object ferociously, to the point that it becomes funny to watch. When he fails to let go, however, despite your trying to wrestle the monster away, it can become frightening and should send up a red flag that your boy needs immediate, strong correction.

Children should be taught never to approach or pick up a Russell who is demonstrating aggressive behavior, for example, toward a mop or a toy, no matter how comical the scene may look. The dog can be so fixated on the object that, when startled by the child, he could snap back. He won't mean to hurt the child, but in an aggressive state, he simply doesn't make the distinction between the child and the object of his attack.

The Russell with Cats

Forget what you've seen on television or in the movies! Generally, the pairing of a Russell and a cat is analogous to walking through a minefield. At any moment, a potentially lethal explosion can occur. Russells seem to have a special dislike reserved for felines. Once a Russell makes an enemy, it's an enemy for life. Even if the Russell appears to give a cat a wide berth, don't

trust the two of them alone. Remember, the Russell was bred to hunt fox. Being the clever, adaptable creature that he is, in the absence of a fox, a cat will do equally well!

Does this mean that a Russell and a cat, even if raised together, will grow to be mortal enemies? Not at all; they could become the best of friends. But even friends have been known to get into squabbles, and in this case, the cat would be on the losing end of the altercation. You have to ask yourself if the risk is worth it.

Breed Truths

Many owners initially underestimate the agility of the Russell because he is small in size. In fact, he is more than capable of jumping as high as five or more feet off the ground and of using his paws to open drawers, and refrigerators. Some can even figure out how to undo childproof clasps!

The Russell with Small Mammals

Again, you need only to refer to the history and function of the breed to realize that pet rodents like mice, gerbils, hamsters, and ferrets are an invitation for your Russell to go on a hunt: through the house, in the yard, in the garage, or wherever the unsuspecting victims are caged. No matter how safely they may be confined, your Russell will have one recurring dream: to pillage and plunder their living quarters and get his prey!

The Russell and Obedience

In the dog world, the Russell's IQ is over the charts. Because of to his high level of intelligence, people automatically presume that he will adapt to training easily. This is usually not true. Although he has the smarts to know what you want him to do, he also thinks he has a better way of doing it.

Have you ever tried to convince an opinionated person that you're right and they're wrong? That's approximately what it's like to get your Russell to listen. But once you get his attention, break through his barrier of willfulness, and earn his respect, there are few dogs with as much training potential as the Russell.

Helpful Hints

Your Russell will be in doggy heaven if you enroll in an earth dog club, which sponsors *go to ground* trials where terriers are allowed to dig and tunnel after small critters who are thoroughly secured in sturdy cages so they can't be harmed by the dogs.

The very same qualities that make him stubborn and exasperating, when properly directed, can also make him obedient and a joy to live with. Many owners remark that living with a properly trained Russell is like having another human buddy in the house. The Russell becomes so attuned to his owner's needs that he can almost anticipate what you want before you ask for it.

Expect to put in substantial time and effort before your Russell reaches that level, however. It will take quite a bit of patience and understanding. The road promises to be challenging and frustrating at times, but if you stick with it, the results will be worth all the effort. You'll have an intelligent, respectful, and engaging companion for life.

BE PREPARED! Ground Rules

Setting ground rules for your Russell will help him understand what you expect of him.

- Establish boundaries. As soon as your puppy or adult Russell comes home, teach him what behavior is acceptable and what is not by rewarding good behavior and ignoring inappropriate behavior. Punishment is not an effective method and could lead to aggressive behavior.
- Assume the role of pack leader. Because of his working terrier heritage, the Russell understands this concept above all others. Once he recognizes that *you* are the pack leader, he will assume a subordinate role in the family pack.
- Be consistent. Use the same commands and system of rewards. If you do, your Russell will learn what is expected of him and what is inappropriate.

Remember, above all, your Russell wants to please you. It's up to you to show him how to accomplish that goal. Even though the unique intelligence and energy of the Russell can be challenging, this little dog will also make you laugh when he's happy and cry when he's not. Therefore, the Russell owner must be ready to make a long-term commitment to obedience training to keep you both smiling.

The Russell needs to have complete balance of body and mind to fulfill his breed purpose and be otherwise happy and content. This requires a setting where he will have lots of opportunity for exercise and human companionship.

No matter how much you may fall in love with this little tyke at first sight, as practically all prospective owners do, if your lifestyle is such that he will be left alone or crated for long hours at time, don't invite the Russell into your life. This is a dog whose activity level demands an owner who cannot only provide love and companionship, but also consistently devote the time and energy that living with a Russell necessitates. Do not attempt to rewrite his genetic makeup to fit your way of life or you will both be miserable and disappointed. The Russell is an inimitable dog who needs to have a purpose and a positive outlet for his brain and his brawn to be a happy, healthy, and contented member of the family.

Fun Facts

Russells want your companionship 24/7. If you aren't paying enough attention to your little super-dog, don't be surprised if he sits himself directly in front of you and barks up a storm until you do!

Like most humans, your Russell loves to have a daily routine. It keeps his mind active and focused, so let him tag along when you go to buy the newspaper, take your daily stroll, do the wash, pick up the mail, tidy up the house, and so on. After a few times, you'll be amazed to see how he has the routine memorized!

Ten Simple Rules for Living with a Russell

- Be the pack leader.
- Respect and address the Russell's breed imperatives.
- Enroll him in obedience class.
- Be patient; never use corporal punishment.
- Be positive; use praise.
- Give him daily exercise.
- Give him a daily routine.
- Give him meaningful activity to challenge his mind.
- Socialize him early on.
- Have a fenced yard or a place for him to run.

Chapter Six

Health and Nutrition

Keeping your dog healthy and happy is the most important responsibility you will have as a Parson Russell Terrier owner. It's also a challenge because your Russell can't tell you what's wrong when he's feeling under the weather or just plain sick. As a vigilant owner, it will be up to you to read his body language and notice anything that appears to be out of the ordinary. Sometimes changes are very subtle. Unlike humans, animals tend to tolerate pain and discomfort for a long time before complaining. Unless a dog is in severe pain, he probably won't whine and cry. For example, if your normally active Russell suddenly sits quietly by your chair instead of bringing you his favorite toy to play, you should suspect that there's a reason. He could be in pain. Any behavior that isn't normal for your Russell should be investigated.

Is Your Russell Healthy?

One of the ways to make sure your Russell stays in the peak of health is to make it a practice to "go over" him on a weekly basis. Be aware of his daily habits. If you notice a change, it could signal a problem. Observe his general appearance. Is his weight good, or does he look like he may have lost a pound or two? Is he is alert, energetic, and happy, or is he acting a bit withdrawn and sluggish? Is he moving well, without hesitation, or is he favoring one leg or foot? Does he rush to his food bowl as soon as you put it down or is he disinterested? You can also tell how your Russell is feeling by giving him a quick examination.

Nose Your Russell's nose should be moist and cool to the touch. Don't be alarmed if your dog's nose changes color from black to a muddy brown when the weather gets cold. That's perfectly normal. Feel his nose. If it's hot and dry, he may be running a fever. Also examine his nostrils for any discharge.

Eyes Your Russell's eyes should be bright and clean without discharge. His pupils should be the same size. If you notice a bluish or cloudy cast, he could have cataracts. Bluish eyes that are also bloodshot can signal glaucoma.

Ears Your Russell's ears should be pinkish and odor free. You can use a soft, moist, unscented cloth to wipe the inside of his ear flap. If they smell bad,

or appear reddish, or if he shakes his head or tries to rub the side of his face, he may have an infection or wax buildup. If your dog is out in the woods or romps in the field a lot, he can also pick up parasites as well as burrs and other irritants.

Teeth Your Russell's teeth should be clean and white without any tartar buildup around the gums. His gums should be pink and his breath fresh. If his gums are reddish and puffy with accompanying bad breath, he needs a dental checkup to assess the condition of his gums.

Legs and Body Go over your Russell's legs and body and check for any lumps, bumps, sores, or swelling. Also check him for fleas and ticks. A working Russell or a Russell who spends a good deal of time outdoors must be checked for ticks daily, even though you use a preventive.

Feet and Nails Check the pads of your Russell's feet and make sure there are no cracks, cuts, or foreign objects imbedded. Again, if your Russell is an active working or hunting dog, his feet need special attention on a regular basis. Don't forget to examine the area between his toes. Also be alert for any sores or burns between the toes. Make sure his nails have not become torn or ragged, and always keep them properly clipped.

Skin and Coat Your Russell's coat should be clean, glossy, and free of dandruff. Check his skin for scabs, rashes, redness, or flakiness.

Tail Your Russell's tail should be firm and free of any lumps.

Temperature Your Russell's normal temperature is 100–102.5°F. Use a rectal thermometer to obtain a reading.

Heart Rate Your Russell's heart rate should be between 120 and 160 beats per minute. To check his heartbeat, feel of the left side his chest, under his elbow. Count the number of beats for

Helpful Hints

You can check your Russell's circulation by firmly pressing the gum above his canine tooth with your index finger. The spot you press will turn pale with pressure. Stop pressing. If the pink color does not return to the gum in two or three seconds, he could have circulatory problems.

HOME BASICS
How to Tell If Your Russell Has Ingested a Poison

Many common household products, food, and medicines can be poisonous to your Russell. Learn to recognize the symptoms of poisoning. If you suspect your Russell has ingested one of the following substances, get him to the veterinarian ASAP.

Poison	Symptoms
Antifreeze: Animals are attracted to this dangerous poison due to its sweet taste.	Vomiting and excessive salivating almost immediately after ingestion; staggering, weakness, diarrhea, convulsions; causes kidney failure and often results in death
Barbiturates, ibuprofen, Tylenol, cold tablets: Never leave medicines on tables or anywhere except locked in a medicine cabinet.	Loss of consciousness, shallow breathing, rapid, weak pulse, gray to bluish gums and mucous membranes
Chocolate: Dogs love the taste of chocolate, but it can be deadly.	Vomiting, diarrhea, restlessness, hyperactivity, arrhythmia
Insecticides: These contain nerve toxins.	Some vomiting, followed by listlessness, pale mucous membranes, bloody urine and sometimes bloody diarrhea
Rat poison: Contains coumarin or warfain sodium, both of which are poisonous and impact blood clotting.	Some vomiting, followed by listlessness, caused by internal bleeding, pale mucous membranes, bloody urine and occasionally bloody diarrhea
Snail/slug bait: Contains metaldehyde, a nerve poison, often found on grass.	Excessive salivation within a hour of ingestion, vomiting, diarrhea, staggering, incoordination, stiffness, high fever

15 seconds and then multiply that by 4. You can also check his heart rate by gently pressing his femoral artery, high up in the groin area of his thigh.

Preventive Care

The best way to keep your boy Jack in tip-top condition is to be proactive and take measures to prevent diseases and illnesses before they happen. That means keeping your Russell's vaccinations current and taking him for annual checkups, where your veterinarian will perform a variety of tests and procedures to ensure that your pet will stay in optimum good health.

FYI: Canine Disease and Vaccine Guidelines

Disease	Description	Transmission
Rabies	Viral, affects brain and spinal cord	Body fluids of infected animal penetrate broken skin, mucous membrane, mouth, nose, or eyes of animals or humans
Distemper	Multisystemic, severe disease	Virus, through contact with bodily secretions of infected animals; can also be airborne
Parvovirus	Known as "dog-flu," a deadly viral disease, causes severe dehydration, gastrointestinal and possible heart damage in young puppies	Through ingested feces; has a three-ten day incubation; virus can live for months outside its host
Adenovirus-2	Virus, contagious but rare, seen in combination with other agents that cause upper respiratory infections	Contact with infected animals; can also be airborne; bodily secretions
Parainfluenza	Virus; a type of kennel cough	Airborne
Leptospirosis	Bacteria; causes acute infection that may lead to kidney or liver disease	Contact with urine of an infected host

Vaccinations

In 2006, the American Animal Hospital Association (AAHA) Vaccine Task Force published updated guidelines for vaccine administration. Core vaccines such as distemper, parvovirus, and adenovirus-2, a hepatitis and respiratory infection, are given once and until recently were boosted yearly.

Symptoms	Prognosis	Vaccination
Progressive changes in behavior: nervousness, restlessness, viciousness, biting, frothing at the mouth, bloody saliva, vocal cord paralysis	Death; there is no cure	Puppy vaccination; revaccination at one year old, then every one to three years, depending on local ordinances (core)
Cold-like: nasal discharge, red eyes, vomiting, diarrhea, fever with neurological involvement, i.e., convulsions	Half of infected adult dogs and three quarters of infected puppies die; survivors can develop fatal or chronic nervous-system disorders	Puppy vaccination, then revaccinate at one year old and every three years thereafter (core)
Bloody diarrhea, vomiting, high fever, loss of appetite, depression, can attack the heart causing congestive heart failure	Usually fatal in puppies, especially if not treated immediately; adult dogs have a 50/50 change of survival with treatment	Puppy vaccination, then revaccinate at one year old and every three years thereafter (core)
Dry, hacking cough	Poor to good, depending on the dog's age and general condition	Puppy vaccination, then revaccinate at one year old, and every three years thereafter (core)
Nasal discharge, cough, often with a gagging sound	Good, only lasts a few weeks with treatment; can be serious if left untreated or a secondary bacterial infection presets	Puppy vaccination, then revaccinate at one year old and every year or on an as needed basis thereafter – (non-core)
Loss of appetite, joint pain, fever, depression, nausea, excessive drinking, bleeding	Can cause death; leads to liver or kidney disease if left untreated	Puppy vaccination, then revaccinate at one year old and every year thereafter, or on an as needed basis (non-core)

However, current protocols call for boosters every three years. The exception is the rabies booster, which can be given annually or every three years, depending on local ordinances. Non-core vaccines such as those for Lyme disease, bordetella, and leptospirosis are recommended more frequently or on an "as needed" basis.

Lyme Disease

Unvaccinated Russells are more likely to contract Lyme disease than many other breeds because they tend to spend a great deal of time in the outdoors, particularly in wooded areas. It's important to know the signs so you can take immediate action if you suspect your boy has been infected.

- Lameness or stiffness
- Swelling of limbs or joints
- Fever
- Lethargy or reluctance to move
- Loss of appetite
- Vomiting
- Depression

These signs can also be symptoms of other diseases, but if you observe any of them in your Russell, contact your veterinarian immediately.

Once your Russell is current on all his necessary vaccinations, the next step in preventive health care is to keep your boy free of common parasites, which are broken down into internal and external parasites.

Breed Needs

If your Russell will be spending time in woods and fields, he should receive a yearly Lyme disease vaccination. Depending on where you live, he may need an annual Lyme booster regardless. Certain parts of the country have a greater incidence of ticks than others. Consult with your veterinarian. Furthermore, if you also show your Russell, work him, compete in agility or go-to-ground trials, hunt with him, or board him regularly he should also receive a bordetella booster yearly or as needed. Again, ask your veterinarian for a recommendation.

Internal Parasites

The most common internal parasites are whipworms, roundworms, hookworms, tapeworms, and heartworms. Except for heartworms, these parasites are detected through a fecal examination performed by your veterinarian. Breeders begin this process by worming puppies at two to three weeks of age. A follow-up worming is necessary two weeks after that. If worms are detected in the feces, a third worming is performed. Once your puppy matures, your veterinarian will check for worms during the annual examination. However, if your Russell is a working terrier, he should be checked more often. Even if you don't work or hunt your Rusell, he still loves to play in the grass and dig in the dirt, so he is more likely to come in contact with these parasites than most other breeds.

Whipworms Adult whipworms live in the dog's large intestine and feed on his blood. Eggs are passed through the feces and can live in the soil for years! Your Russell can pick up this parasite by digging or chewing on grass in an infected area. Symptoms of whipworm infestation are watery or bloody diarrhea. It can be difficult to detect in a fecal sample because the worms don't shed eggs continuously. Thus, you may have to bring several specimens to the veterinarian before a diagnosis can be made.

Roundworms Puppies are more likely to be infected with roundworms than adult dogs. The reason is that they are passed to him from the dam if she has ever been infected, and practically every dog has at one time or another. These parasites pass to the puppy through the dam's milk while he is nursing.

Hookworms This parasite is also passed to a puppy through his dam's milk during the first two to three weeks of life. Hookworms are insidious; they literally "hook" onto the wall of the intestine and suck the dog's blood, causing a bloody diarrhea. They are then passed through the feces. A puppy left untreated can die.

Tapeworms Most dog owners are familiar with this pesky parasite, which, unlike the others, is transmitted by the bite of a flea or by swallowing an infected flea. However, it's not uncommon for a Russell to pick up this parasite by coming in contact with or killing rodents or other animals when he's outdoors or going to ground. Tapeworms are visible in your Russell's stool, so be on the lookout. When released, they resemble small grains of white rice. They may also be detected in the hair around your dog's anus. If you see tapeworms, call your veterinarian. Tapeworm infestation can lead to anemia.

Heartworms Heartworms are thin, spaghetti-like worms that can grow up to 12 inches long. They live inside the dog's heart, and for that reason they must be treated immediately or congestive heart failure can result.

Infection begins when a mosquito carrying heartworm larvae bites your dog. The larvae then burrow beneath his skin and molt two times, eventually emerging as immature worms inside the body. This process takes between 50 and 68 days. Once the heartworms mature, they travel through the dog's bloodstream and settle in the right ventricle and pulmonary arteries. Heartworms mature in about six months and can live as long as five years. Dogs with a heavy heartworm infestation may have as many as 250 worms. But even a few are too many.

Luckily, you can prevent your Russell from ever getting this dangerous parasite by having the veterinarian perform a simple blood test once a year. If it is negative, the veterinarian will put your dog on heartworm preventive medication, which he will need to take monthly during the mosquito season. However, if your Russell spends a good deal of time outdoors in swampy areas, or if you work or hunt him, you should keep him on heartworm preventive meds all year-round. This is also true if you are actively showing your Russell and have to travel to different parts of the country with him. But even if the only time your dog spends outside is when you walk or exercise him, he still needs to be on heartworm preventive because there's a good chance he'll become infected without treatment. It's that common. If your Russell does become infected with heartworms, he has a very good chance of a full recovery, but only with treatment, which can be quite expensive.

CAUTION

Do not put your Russell on heartworm preventive medication without having him tested first. If he has already been infected, all the medication will do is kill immature heartworms while the mature worms live on, unaffected, and your dog's health deteriorates.

External Parasites

Fleas, ticks, and mites are some of the common external parasites that love your Russell even more than you do! And why not? Your furry boy provides an ideal place for them to get all the food they need, and to get all warm and cozy, too! Summer and fall are typically the seasons when external parasites strike. The Russell is at an even greater risk than most dog breeds for infestation because he spends so much time outside. But guess what? When he comes into the house, so do the pesky parasites, some of which can be passed on to the human members of the household. You must be proactive. The best mode of attack is to prevent fleas and ticks from using your pet as a host.

There are a number of ways to flea-and tick-proof your Russell. Topical monthly treatments like Frontline and Advantage are both convenient and quite effective, without causing side effects. There are also flea dips and powders, which must be used judiciously because they can be toxic if your dog licks himself after application. If you select this method of treatment, it's best to ask your veterinarian for the safest and most effective product.

As an added line of defense, there are several borax-based products that can be swept into your carpets and furniture. They function to break the life cycle of the flea so that it cannot reproduce and thus cause an infestation in your home. Sometimes it is also necessary to treat your yard if there is a severe infestation.

Fleas Fleas are hard to see because they are not only tiny but also move exceedingly fast and, yes, they even jump! If you notice your Russell scratching and biting at his skin, you can be fairly certain that a flea is the culprit. Some dogs develop a flea allergy. In this case, the saliva from the bite of the flea will cause inflammation and even more irritation for your pet. Fleas also multiply at an alarmingly rapid rate. Thus, when your dog picks up a single flea and comes into the house, that flea will lay hundreds of eggs in your carpet, and furniture, and in no time, your home will be infested with these hardy critters. For this reason, preventing fleas is the first and best defense.

Ticks Ticks come in various small sizes from the minuscule deer tick to the larger brown dog tick. They affect dogs during the summer and fall and are commonly found in warm, grassy, and wooded areas. Again, the Russell is more likely to pick up ticks because of his need to be outdoors. Certain tick bites can be very harmful to your dog and cause irritation, hypersensitivity, skin damage, and anemia. Ticks can also carry Rocky Mountain spotted fever and Lyme disease. Both diseases can be very dangerous if left untreated. Unlike fleas, ticks are fairly easy to spot on your pet. They feel like tiny bumps on the surface of the skin. Generally they burrow into the dog's skin on the limbs, around the head and neck, and on the ears. If you take your Russell out for a jaunt in the woods or a run in a field, check his skin when you get home for any sign of ticks.

Helpful Hints

If you discover a tick on your Russell, it's important to remove it correctly. Do this by first dabbing it with a cotton swab soaked in alcohol. Next, take a tweezers and grasp the tick as close to your dog's skin as possible. Then pull it out slowly, without twisting or jerking. Make sure you have removed the whole tick, including the head. After removing the tick, place it in a sealed jar with alcohol. It's a good idea to bring it to your veterinarian so he can test it for disease. Treat the area of the tick bite on your dog with alcohol or other disinfectant. If you are unable to remove the tick, take your Russell to the veterinarian. Do not allow a tick to remain on your dog!

Mites The most common type of mite is the ear mite. These parasites are easy to recognize because they leave a brown or black crust on the outer ear. If you notice your dog scratching or rubbing his ear area, check the ear for mites. Scabies are another type of mite. They burrow under the skin's surface where they lay eggs, which, in turn, cause intense itching and irritation. Scabies are also highly contagious, so if you suspect that you Russell has them, bring him to the veterinarian as soon as possible.

Inherited and Congenital Weaknesses

Cerebellar Ataxia This neurological disease results from degeneration of the cortex of the cerebellum. It causes the dog to stagger or appear to wobble when he walks. Another common symptom is disorientation.

Cruciate Ligament Rupture All highly athletic dogs are prone to this type of injury. It occurs when a ligament in the knee tears, making the thighbone slide back and forth over the shinbone, creating an extreme pain that eventually leads to arthritis. Sometimes this type of a rupture will repair itself with proper rest, but it usually requires surgery.

Legg-Calve-Perthes Disease This degenerative disease affects small dogs, and the Russell is considered at a higher risk than other breeds. The disease, which is inherited, is a degeneration of the head of the thighbone, and results in progressive lameness. It rarely manifests itself before a puppy is four months old. Surgery is recommended to correct the problem and the prognosis is good.

Hip and Elbow Dysplasia Dysplasia occurs when the head of the bone no longer fits into the cup provided by the socket, causing lameness and arthritis-like symptoms. Reputable breeders should have all their breeding stock OFA (Orthopedic Foundation for Animals) tested.

Hypothyroidism Caused by an underactive thyroid gland, hypothyroidism can cause a decreased appetite or weight gain, hair loss, recurring skin infections, and lethargy.

Breed Truths

Although the Russell is generally strong, healthy, and long-lived, the breed does have a predisposition to certain diseases and medical conditions. These problems can either be inherited or congenital and develop at a young or old age. However, just because these conditions are seen in some Russells, it does not mean that your dog will ever be affected. Nonetheless, you should be aware of common weaknesses seen in the breed and if you suspect your puppy is symptomatic, consult with your veterinarian.

Lens Luxation This commonly inherited disease involves the dislocation of the lens in one or both eyes. Depending on the degree of the luxation, it can be painful and the eye can look red or swollen. The condition shows up in older dogs and must be treated right away to avoid blindness. Breeders should have their breeding stock certified by the Canine Eye Registry Foundation (CERF).

Cataracts Hereditary cataracts commonly affect Russells. A cataract is any abnormal cloudiness of the eye's lens. The cataract can be just a small spot or it can be more diffuse. Inherited cataracts can affect young adult dogs and develop slowly over several years. They can also be caused by diabetes, trauma to the eye, infection, and shock. Cataracts don't affect vision immediately, but as the condition progresses, the dog could lose sight in the affected eye. Surgery, when performed early on, can restore vision.

Deafness Congenital deafness is a significant problem for the Parson Russell Terrier. It can be unilateral (affecting one ear) or bilateral (affecting both ears). The Brainstem Auditory Evoked Response (BAER) test is available to puppies over five weeks of age. Your breeder should have this test performed on all puppies that are to be sold. Be sure to ask the breeder if his or her puppies have a BAER certificate.

Congestive Heart Failure Russells are prone to CHF, which is caused by a leaky heart valve and produces a heart murmur. It can also be caused by another condition called cardiomyopathy, which is characterized by a weakened heart muscle. Symptoms of CHF are coughing, wheezing, labored breathing, and weight loss.

Von Wildebrand Disease Also known as vWD, this is an inherited breeding disorder, characterized by abnormal platelet function. Common symptoms are bleeding from the nose and gums, bloody urine, excessive post-op bleeding, or prolonged bleeding after cutting too closely when trimming your dog's nails. Breeders generally advertise their litters as being vWD free after testing.

Sarcoptic Mange Though neither hereditary or inherited, a working Russell is a prime candidate to contract this disease, which is caused by a mite. A Russell can contract sarcoptic mange by entering earth where a fox or any other animal with the disease has stayed. Even puppies playing in holes can pick up mange. The disease is highly contagious and usually appears on the face first and then spreads to other parts of the body. It is characterized by itchy, scabby skin, with missing patches of hair. Humans can also contract this disease.

Signs Your Russell Is Ill

Unfortunately your beloved companion can't talk and tell you when he's not feeling well. It's up to you to observe his behavior and body language and decide if he needs to see the veterinarian. Some conditions need immediate attention, whereas others may correct themselves within a 24-hour period. The following guidelines will help you differentiate an emergency situation from something less serious.

Emergency—Contact Your Veterinarian Immediately If Your Russell:
- has no pulse or heartbeat;
- is not breathing or is having extreme difficulty breathing;
- has pale or bluish gums or tongue;
- has a broken bone or cut where the bone is exposed
- is bleeding profusely;
- has been hit by a moving vehicle;
- has an eye injury where the eye is enlarged, protruding, or out of its socket;

- has been in a fight with a wild or unvaccinated animal;
- has received a wound from a bullet or arrow;
- has a puncture wound;
- has been bitten by a snake, scorpion, poisonous spider, or toad;
- has porcupine quills imbedded in any part of his body;
- has a severe laceration or an incision that has opened;
- has heatstroke or a fever above 105°F;
- has frostbite or hypothermia;
- is choking or vomiting blood;
- has a bloated abdomen;
- is unconscious or disoriented;
- has a seizure;
- is suddenly unable to stand or walk;
- is unable to urinate or cries when trying to urinate; or
- is bleeding from the genital area.

Non-emergency—Contact Your Veterinarian After 24 Hours If Your Russell:

- is sneezing or coughing;
- has some respiratory difficulty;
- has not eaten or consumed any water;
- has had vomiting or diarrhea for 24 hours;
- is drinking excessive amounts of water, unrelated to any physical activity or increased outside temperature;
- has a sudden change in behavior;
- cries when touched or picked up;
- has sudden lameness;
- has a nosebleed;
- is lethargic and depressed;
- has swollen joints or lumps; or
- has discharge from the eyes, nose, or any bodily opening.

CAUTION

NEVER put yourself between two fighting dogs. Dogs in fight mode, even a loving family pet, will bite anything or anyone that tries to interfere. During a moment of high adrenaline rush like this, your dog will not even be aware that he's biting you when you try to separate him and the other fighting dog.

Dog Bites

Parson Russell Terriers have a reputation for being dog aggressive. Even if your Russell is as mild as a lamb, he may encounter another dog he doesn't particularly like or one that doesn't like him, and a fight may ensue. He could also be attacked and bitten by another dog while you're out walking him. If your dog is bitten, get him and yourself to a safe place as soon as possible, without getting bitten yourself.

CHECKLIST

First Aid Kit

Always keep a first aid kit handy at home in case of an emergency. Because you and your Russell will probably go on hikes and other adventures together, you should also keep a second kit in your car. The following items should be included:

✔ Gauze sponges
✔ Nonstick bandages
✔ First aid tape, nonstick and adhesive
✔ Stretch gauze bandage rolls
✔ Cotton swabs
✔ Cotton balls
✔ Soft muzzle
✔ Wound disinfectant, such as Betadine
✔ Karo syrup
✔ Nutritional supplement, such as Nutri-Cal
✔ Gatorade or other rehydrating solution
✔ Bottled water
✔ Triple antibiotic ointment, such as Neosporin
✔ Ophthalmic antibiotic solution, such as Terramycin
✔ Eye wash solution
✔ Anti-itch spray, such as Benedryl or Cortaid
✔ Hydrocortisone cream (10%)
✔ Benedryl allergy capsules (25 mg)
✔ Buffered or canine aspirin
✔ Cold and heat packs (wrap in towel before applying)

✔ Rubbing alcohol
✔ Petroleum Jelly
✔ Soap
✔ Ear flush
✔ Pepto Bismol, Kaopectate tablets (maximum strength)
✔ Antidiarrheal
✔ Hydrogen peroxide
✔ Sterile saline solution
✔ Activated charcoal to absorb ingested poisons (consult your veterinarian before using)
✔ Hydrocortisone acetate—1% cream
✔ Styptic powder, such as Kwik Stop
✔ Magnifying glass
✔ Splints
✔ Blanket
✔ Scissors
✔ Tweezers
✔ Rectal thermometer
✔ Nail clippers and metal nail file
✔ Eye dropper or oral syringe
✔ Ziplock bags
✔ Disposable gloves
✔ Syringes of various sizes
✔ Blankets
✔ Flashlight
✔ Veterinarian's phone number
✔ Emergency clinic phone number
✔ Poison control center phone numbers
✔ Dog's health records, including vaccinations

If the other dog is with his owner, get contact information and find out if the other dog is current with all of his shots, particularly rabies, as well as the name of his veterinarian. Take your dog to your veterinarian immediately so he can be treated and evaluated.

Bite wounds are among the most common emergencies seen in veterinary emergency hospitals. A bite wound can be simple and require only cleaning or more serious requiring sutures, X-rays, medication, and even hospitalization. Depending on the severity, a dog can die from bite wounds.

Dental Care

CAUTION

Proper dental hygiene is another preventive measure you can take to keep your Russell in top condition. Your Russell has 42 permanent teeth by the time he is four months old. Just like humans, he needs regular dental care to keep his teeth and gums healthy and free from infection and

Do not ever give your Russell animal bones, thinking they will keep his teeth clean. They can splinter and cause internal bleeding and choking.

decay. Alarmingly, periodontal disease is becoming more and more common in young dogs, largely because owners don't realize that dogs also need to practice oral hygiene. Tartar builds up quickly, especially around canine teeth and upper molars. If you work your Russell, he's prone to missing or broken teeth and abscesses, so be very vigilant.

Begin dental care when your Russell is a puppy. If you get him used to having his teeth brushed at an early age, not only will he have good teeth, but he'll also readily accept having his mouth worked on as he matures.

HOME BASICS
Keeping Your Russell's Teeth and Gums Healthy

1. Try to brush your Russell's teeth daily, or at the very least, once a week.

2. Start by using a child's toothbrush or a specially designed finger brush, which will get him used to having his teeth and gums massaged; work up to an angled dog toothbrush which you can purchase in a pet store, from a catalog or from your veterinarian;

3. Use special dog toothpaste, not human toothpaste. Dogs swallow the paste, rather than spitting it out like humans, so it must be digestible.

4. Use a circular motion, which will clean the teeth and massage the gums as well.

5. If you don't brush your Russell's teeth daily, give him a dental chew instead. Select a dental chew containing enzymes, which keep breath fresh and control plaque.

6. You can also use specially formulated dog mouth rinses and gels to supplement brushing.

7. Some dog foods are specially formulated to address oral hygiene, such as Science Diet.

Symptoms of Dental Disease
The following may indicate that your Russell has a dental problem:

- bad breath
- pain in and around the mouth
- facial swelling
- dropping food
- reluctance to eat dry food or biscuits
- increased salivation

If you notice one or a combination of these symptoms, call your veterinarian and schedule a dental check.

Pet Insurance

With the cost of animal health care nearly rivaling that of human health care, it's a wise investment to enroll your Russell in a good pet insurance program. If you get your Russell as a puppy, enroll him then, as premiums are less expensive. There are several good pet insurance companies, offering a variety of levels of coverage. If your Russell is AKC registered, the AKC has an insurance program as well. Depending on the insurance carrier you choose, many programs are all-inclusive, covering yearly checkups, vaccinations, medication, emergency situations, accidents, and a host of diseases,

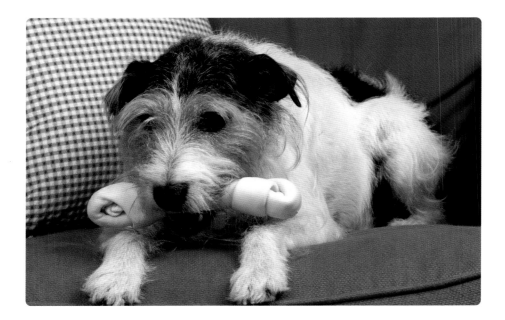

even cancer. Other programs have deductibles. You are free to select the coverage that you think will be right for you and your pet. Some plans do not include dental insurance, which may require a special rider. All in all, having pet insurance will give you peace of mind that your boy will always be able to receive the necessary medical care he needs at any stage in his life.

Russell Nutrition

Keeping your Russell free of disease or other illnesses is only one half of the profile for a healthy, happy dog. The other essential component to his well-being is to ensure that he gets proper nutrition. In fact, many diseases and illnesses in both man and companion animals can be traced to poor nutrition. Remember the old adage "You are what you eat?" Modern medicine is proving that not only is this true, but proper nutrition and eating habits can greatly enhance and prolong life. Feeding your Russell a high-quality dog food specifically formulated for his stage in life and his activity level is the best way to accomplish that.

Your Russell requires certain nutrients in his diet. They include water, protein, carbohydrates, fatty acids, minerals, and vitamins.

Water

Water is the most important nutrient because it allows your Russell's cells to function. The body of an adult dog is composed of 60 percent water. It hydrates his body. A dog deprived of water will die sooner than one deprived

FYI: Protein and Kidney Disease

There has been quite a bit of misinformation about protein and kidney disease in dogs. Until recently it was widely believed that too much protein in a dog's diet, particularly an older dog, could lead to kidney disease. In fact, many dogs with renal dysfunction are put on diets containing high-quality protein derived from eggs, poultry, and meat. High protein levels *do not* cause kidney damage in the normal, healthy dog. Although there is still no magic number for the amount of protein needed in a canine diet, animal nutritionists and veterinarians generally agree that a healthy dog can easily handle a diet containing at least 30 percent animal protein on a dry weight basis, derived from meat and meat by-products. If you purchase a high-quality dog food, it should contain meat as the main ingredient. This will provide the right amount of protein for your Russell. Also contrary to popular belief, senior dogs should not be put on lower-protein diets just because of age. In fact, some older pets require a diet higher in protein than when they were youngsters. Unless your veterinarian advises otherwise, you should always provide your Russell with high-quality protein in his diet.

of food! Your Russell gets water from drinking and from the food he eats. He also gets something called *metabolic water* from the breakdown of the fats, carbohydrates, and proteins that he consumes. Some water is lost throughout the day through the passing of urine and feces as well as through breathing, panting, and illnesses like diarrhea, vomiting, and kidney disease. If it's very hot outside, if your Russell has had a great deal of exercise, or if he has been working in the field, he will lose an excessive amount of water. Your Russell should always have access to clean, fresh water.

CAUTION

A high-energy dog like the Russell can easily become dehydrated through heavy exercise, working, or other endurance activities, especially in hot or humid weather. Dehydration can set in rapidly and cause shock, coma, and ultimately death. To avoid this, always carry a bottle of water or Gatorade for your Russell when you take him on an outing or even a long walk.

Protein

Proteins are chemicals made up of other chemicals called amino acids. Amino acids are used to synthesize hormones, enzymes, body secretions, and other body proteins. They are divided into two groups: essential amino acids (those the dog can't manufacture or synthesize and thus must get in his diet) and nonessential amino acids (those that he can manufacture in his body). Proteins from animal sources like meat and meat by-products are more complete and easier for the dog to extract and digest than proteins derived from plant sources. Proteins are important because they form the enzymes that metabolize food into energy and the hormones that direct different bodily functions. Proteins themselves can also be metabolized to provide energy. High-quality-protein dog foods are recommended for puppies and throughout the life of your adult Russell.

Carbohydrates

Sugars, dietary fibers, and starches collectively make up carbohydrates. Your Russell's diet should consist of about 50 percent carbohydrates. The source of carbohydrates is an important consideration. The most popular and commonly used in commercial dog foods are corn and soybeans. Other sources include rice, wheat, and potato starch. Some of the premium dog foods, particularly wellness and holistic-based formulas, use more exotic carbs. However, as long as the carbohydrate source is clean and of a good nutritional quality, it probably doesn't matter. Some dogs may be allergic to one or more of these sources, and others may experience bloating or flatulence on soybean formulas, for example, but the majority of dogs do well on most sources of carbohydrate.

Helpful Hints

During the winter months when you have the heat on in your house, the air can become dry, and that can cause your Russell's skin to become dry and itchy. You can alleviate this condition by adding omega fatty acids to his diet as a supplement.

Fats

Dietary fat represents a concentrated source of energy. Fats supply your dog with more than twice as much energy as he gets from either proteins or carbohydrates. They also supply him with essential fatty acids. Contrary to popular belief, fats are not the cause of obesity. However, a food high in fat will cause obesity in a low-energy dog. This is usually not a problem with the Russell, who needs fats for general good health. In addition, fats make dog food more palatable. They also are essential for healthy coat, skin, and kidney function.

Vitamins

Your Russell needs vitamins and minerals in proper balance and ratio in order to remain in good health. Vitamins and minerals are necessary for absorption of fats and carbohydrates and for the chemical reactions in the body. Vitamins are divided into water-soluble and fat-soluble types. Fat-soluble vitamins are stored in fatty tissue, whereas water-soluble vitamins are excreted from the body if unused.

Water-soluble vitamins are all the B-complex vitamins such as thiamine, riboflavin, pantothenic acid, niacin, pyridoxine, biotin, folic acid, choline, and B12. B-vitamins help convert food to energy. Vitamin C is also a water-soluble vitamin, but dogs can manufacture their own supply of vitamin C, so it's not necessary in dog food. However, some breeders are very adamant about supplementing the diet of working Russells with vitamin C because they feel it is essential under stress.

The fat-soluble vitamins are A, D, E, and K. They support many body functions such as eyesight, bone formation, strength (with calcium), cell stability, and blood coagulation. Vitamin K can be synthesized by bacteria in the dog's intestine and does not need to be added to your Russell's diet under ordinary circumstances. Deficiencies of vitamin E can cause muscle tissue breakdown, and can also impair his immune response. Vitamin A deficiency can cause several eye problems, including dryness, corneal ulcerations, and inflammation of the conjunctiva. Vitamin D deficiency causes rickets.

CAUTION

Don't give your Russell vitamin supplements unless they are recommended by your veterinarian. Fat-soluble vitamins, for example, can build up in tissues and become toxic; too much vitamin A can cause bone disease; too much vitamin D can cause calcification of soft tissue, lungs, and kidneys. Although vitamins are good for your dog, too much of a good thing can cause the opposite effect. If you want to give your dog supplements, consult your veterinarian first.

Minerals

Minerals are the major components of bones and teeth and help to maintain the body's acid base, nervous system function, and electrolyte and fluid balances. Minerals are divided into major and trace concentrations.

Major:
- Calcium and phosphorus are necessary for bone formation and strength. An imbalance in their ratio will cause bone problems.
- Potassium, found within tissue cells, is important in cellular activity; a deficiency causes muscle weakness and heart and kidney lesions.
- Sodium, found in fluids outside the tissue cells, performs a function similar to potassium. It is found in the diet as sodium chloride—salt—and is rarely deficient. Too much sodium can cause hypertension in dogs.

- Magnesium, found in soft tissue and bone, interacts with calcium for proper heart, muscle, and nervous tissue function; it also aids in the metabolism of potassium and sodium. Deficiency can cause muscle weakness and sometimes convulsions.

Trace:
- Iron is critical for healthy red blood cells and is an essential component of some enzymes. Deficiency is associated with anemia, which causes weakness and fatigue.
- Zinc is heavily involved in skin and coat health, enzyme function, and protein synthesis. Deficiencies lead to poor growth, anorexia, testicular atrophy, and skin lesions.
- Copper is necessary for the production of melanin, the pigment that colors coat and skin, and is linked with iron metabolism. Deficiencies can cause a bone disorder and anemia even if iron intake is normal.
- Selenium acts in conjunction with Vitamin E to protect cells against damage.
- Manganese: Little is known about specific requirements in dogs.

CAUTION

Store your Russell's food in a sealed container in a cool, dry place. Do not keep food outdoors, as insects and vermin could find their way inside.

What Should You Feed Your Russell?

There are dozens of dog foods on the market, and trying to choose the right one can be daunting. Unlike the average house pet, the Russell is a high-energy dog and as such his nutritional requirements are different. This is especially true if you also work or show your Russell. Puppies require more calories than adults. But not all calories are created equal. It's not a matter of quantity but the quality of calories he's ingesting from the ingredients in his food that will ensure that your boy is getting a well-balanced meal for his age and activity level.

The ingredients, which are listed on the dog food bag, must be in the right combinations and be of good quality both before and after processing. The biological values of these ingredients is the key to good nutrition. The biological value of a food is determined by the amino acid completeness of the proteins the food contains.

Biological Value

Eggs	100%
Fish meal	92%
Beef, chicken lamb, turkey, other meats	78%
Milk	78%
Wheat	69%
Wheat gluten	40%
Corn	54%

Also keep in mind that the U.S. Department of Agriculture does not impose a mandatory inspection of ingredients used in pet food manufacturing. Therefore, before choosing a food for your Russell, conduct your own investigation of the company and manufacturer of the pet food you are considering. Don't go for bargain-basement foods. Make sure the company is reputable, and uses an equally reputable processing facility. Finally, ask for recommendations from your veterinarian and your breeder. Feeding your Russell the best possible food will end up saving you both money and heartache in the long run. Here are some tips to help you choose the best food for your dog.

CAUTION

Remember to always keep fresh water available for your Russell. If he's left alone for long periods during the day, use an automatic watering bowl, which acts similarly to a self-feeder.

The Raw Diet

Many dog owners and breeders are fans of the raw food diet. The reasoning behind this is that animals are carnivores and eat raw kill in the wild. Furthermore, proponents of the raw diet think commercial pet food is over processed and tainted with toxins, which are used to preserve the food and to give it an attractive smell and taste. Raw meat enthusiasts also argue that many commercial pet foods contain numerous toxins that impair the health of the animal, such as sodium nitrate, artificial flavorings, and other impurities. Dogs who eat an all-fresh-food diet are supposed to have better coats, fewer dental problems, and fresher breath. However, there are no clinical

HOME BASICS
How to Choose the Right Dog Food

In selecting a dog food for your Russell, keep in mind the following guidelines:

✔ The food must have the Association of American Feed Control Officials (AAFCO) guarantee on the box or container.

✔ Check for an expiration date. Do not buy food near or beyond the expiration date stamped on the bag or container.

✔ Make sure you buy food that is formulated for the proper life stage of your pet, e.g., puppy, adult, or senior.

✔ Read the label; make sure meat (chicken, beef, turkey, lamb) is the first ingredient, rice is the main grain source, and mixed tocopherols (vitamin E) is the preservative.

✔ If your Russell has special dietary needs, consider feeding either the specially veterinary-formulated foods or feeding a home-made diet that specifically addresses his needs.

✔ Feed your Russell according to the guidelines for his weight posted on the dog food package.

trials to actually back up any of these claims, only the claims of individuals. If you are convinced that a raw diet is best for your Russell, choose one of the commercially available raw food diets that are complete and balanced. They are sold frozen and must be consumed within a short period of time. You can find raw diets at your pet store and through your veterinarian. If you decide to switch to a raw diet, make sure you introduce it gradually into your Russell's feeding schedule. Dogs that are not used to eating raw diets could initially experience gastric upset resulting in vomiting and diarrhea.

The Homemade Diet
Many people choose to feed homemade diets in an effort to replicate the diet nature intended, but this can be time consuming and end up costing more money than commercial food. But more important, you need to supplement any homemade diet with multivitamins and other supplements

CAUTION

Do not attempt to prepare your own homemade raw diet for your pet. Despite your best intentions, it could be dangerous, because if foods are not correctly formulated and balanced, it will lead to nutritional deficiency.

like fatty acids and antioxidants in the right amount and ratio based on your dog's size and metabolic needs. No matter how fresh the homemade diet may be, if it isn't properly balanced to meet your Russell's nutritional needs, it can do him more harm than good. If you're concerned about chemicals

and additives in commercial dog food, you may want to check out natural or holistic dog food companies, which essentially offer the same benefits of a homemade diet without the risks.

Obesity

Obesity has become one of the major health issues in the human population. Not surprisingly, it's also increasing in the pet population. Many well-meaning owners love to pamper their beloved four-legged companions with food and treats all day long, causing their pets to become dangerously overweight. It is estimated that as many as 40 percent of domestic dogs are obese! As with humans, an overweight dog will become lazy and sedentary, creating a vicious cycle of physical problems ranging from diabetes to cardiovascular disease to orthopedic and other metabolic and physical ailments. More is not better. An obese dog, like an obese human, has a compromised quality of life and a shorter life span.

Keep your Russell from overeating by feeding the proscribed amount of food at regular times. Don't get into the habit of feeding him table scraps, cakes, cookies, or other sugar-laden human foods. Not only will it make him fat, but it will harm his teeth. When you want to reward him or just give him a between-meals snack, offer your Russell a high-quality dog biscuit. But don't overdo it and dole out a box of treats every day.

Sometimes, dogs can become overweight because they develop metabolic problems from disorders like diabetes mellitus, hypothyroidism, hyperadrenocorticism (Cushing's disease), hypoadrenocorticism (Addison's disease), and other endocrine abnormalities. If your dog becomes overweight, your veterinarian will probably recommend feeding him a high-fiber reduced-calorie diet and/or suggest other dietary and lifestyle changes like increased exercise.

Unless your Russell has a medical condition that predisposes him to weight gain, there is no reason for him to ever be overweight. If he is, it means you are not giving him the exercise he desperately needs to be a happy, healthy dog! A Russell is not by nature a couch potato. If you try to turn him into one, and he becomes obese and sedentary, he will not be a happy dog or a long-lived one. In fact, allowing a normal, healthy Russell to become overweight is tantamount to animal cruelty, because he is being forced to go against the breed imperative of a true Russell.

Forbidden Food

Chocolate is not the only everyday food that can be toxic to your Russell. Seemingly benign foods like onions, garlic, grapes, raisins, and yes, even the human wonder food, broccoli, can also be poisonous.

Helpful Hints

Your Russell expends a lot of energy on a normal day. For this reason it's a good practice to split up his daily food ration and feed him two to three times a day. This will keep his blood glucose level on track and also prevent him from eating too much in one sitting, which can cause him gastric upset. Don't allow dog food to remain in his bowl for more than 20–30 minutes, especially if it is moistened. What he doesn't consume within that time should be discarded. If you work during the day, you may want to opt for a self-feeder, so your Russell will have his scheduled meals when you are out of the house. Some self-feeders have a timer that releases food according to how you program it. Self-feeders are good only if you feed a dry diet.

- Onions and garlic contain a toxic ingredient called thiosulphate and cause anemia if consumed in large amounts. Garlic, however, can be good for your dog in very small amounts, as it acts as a natural flea repellent.
- Grapes and raisins can cause acute renal (kidney) failure when consumed in large amounts.
- Broccoli contains isothiocyanate, a powerful gastrointestinal irritant that can be very painful. However, in small amounts (less than 5 percent of your Russell's diet) it is highly nutritional and may help prevent cancer.
- Mushrooms can also be toxic and lead to severe digestive problems, neurological disorders, and liver disease. Your Russell loves the outdoors and may take the notion to graze, so make sure you clean your yard of any wild mushrooms.
- Turkey skin is very difficult to digest and has been linked with acute pancreatic disease in dogs.
- Sugar-free candies are toxic.
- Raw salmon is also toxic.

If you think your Russell has ingested any type of poison, whether it be natural, plant, or chemical, *do not* hesitate; call your veterinarian immedi-

FYI: Digestive Problems and Remedies

Are you in a quandary about what to do when your Russell gets a tummy ache?

The following are natural remedies to cure some common problems:

- Pumpkin. For diarrhea, feed it raw from the can, uncooked, and unsweetened. It helps sooth the digestive tract and helps with minor digestive disorders.
- Peas and Carrots. Finicky eater? Spice up your Russell's dry food with these tasty and healthy add-ins.

- Papaya. A digestive aid, its enzymes help in digestion of nutrients, minerals, and vitamins.
- Peppermint leaves. Bad doggy breath? Try adding one or two leaves to your Russell's food.

If any digestive problems persist for more than 24 hours, consult your veterinarian, as they may signal a more serious condition.

ately. You can also call your local poison control center, or call the National Animal Poison Control Center at (900) 680-0000.

The Dangers of Chocolate

It cannot be stressed enough: Chocolate can be lethal to your pet! Most households commonly have comfort items like chocolate chip cookies, chocolate candy, and chocolate brownies lying around on tables or countertops. Remember that your Russell is exceptionally agile and can easily leap as high as a kitchen counter or a breakfast bar to snatch something that is particularly attractive to him. Like humans, all dogs have a sweet tooth. Thus, keeping chocolate in any form within the reach of your Russell is just too tempting for him, and it is one of the *most lethal* substances he can ingest. Many inexperienced dog owners are unaware that even a small amount of chocolate can be deadly. Chocolate contains a naturally occurring stimulant called theobromine, which is found in the cocoa bean plant. It affects both the central nervous system and the heart, essentially sending your dog's system into red-alert mode, which can then manifest itself in the form of epileptic-type seizures. All it may take is *one* chocolate bar or *less*! Consider the fact that your Russell is a small dog and the amount of theobromine present in milk chocolate is approximately 44–60 mg/ounce; in unsweetened baking chocolate it's a whopping 450 mg/ounce!

Fun Facts

Is your Russell a vegan? Although dogs are classified as carnivores, i.e., flesh eaters, they are really omnivorous, meaning they are able to subsist on a mixture of plant and animal tissue. Dogs can thrive on a vegan diet, provided it's carefully formulated and properly balanced. And, always consult your veterinarian before changing your dog's diet.

10 Questions About Health and Nutrition

1 **Sometimes my Russell's stomach makes rumbling noises. What should I do?**
There are many causes for "rumbling" stomach noises. One of the most common is that your dog is hungry. If it isn't close to his mealtime and he doesn't seem interested in food, he could have an intestinal upset. Call your veterinarian and describe the symptoms.

2 **Why does my Russell eat grass?** Sometimes dogs eat grass simply because they like it. Grass eating is also the way your dog cleans out his digestive system. However, grass can also be an irritant to his digestive tract.

3 **How often do I need to trim my dog's nails?** The rule of thumb is that if you can hear your dog's nails tapping on the floor when he walks, his nails need clipping. For some dogs this requires weekly maintenance. Other dogs need less frequent trims. Some dogs never need their nails clipped at all if they constantly walk on abrasive surfaces, like concrete, for example.

4 **My Russell sometimes has a foul odor coming from under his tail. What is that?**
First check to see if your dog has any fecal or other odiferous matter attached to his tail. If this isn't the problem, he may have impacted anal glands. This happens when the two glands on either side of his anus are unable to

expel anal secretion when he has a bowel movement. This causes an impaction, and if not attended to, the glands can become infected. Your veterinarian will have to excise his glands to drain the built-up matter. This is generally a simple process that will make your dog and you feel a lot better afterward.

5 **Sometimes my Russell rubs his eyes and his face with both paws. What is he trying to do?** Constant scratching or rubbing around the face or eyes should be checked out by your veterinarian. Your dog can have anything from an allergy to a foreign object in his eyes or stuck in his gums or between his teeth. Often dogs with periodontal disease or broken teeth will paw at their faces. On the other hand, he may just have an itch.

6 **My Russell has a lot of gas. What can I do about that?**
If you have recently either changed your Russell's dog food or perhaps fed him some people snacks, it could case a digestive upset resulting in intestinal gas. If he has chronic gas, you may need to put him on a new diet. Consult with your veterinarian before taking action.

7 **When my Russell is out in the yard, I'm concerned that he will eat a mouse or other vermin. Is that dangerous?**
A Russell will naturally hunt field mice, possums, and badgers if given the opportunity.

It's what he was bred to do. Generally, they do not eat their kill. However, should your Russell take to munching on a dead mouse or other critter, it's wise to contact your veterinarian immediately and bring a specimen of the carcass with you. Rodents and other wild animals can carry diseases ranging from worms to rabies. If your Russell ingests a dead mouse, there is also a danger of secondary poisoning, if the mouse ingested a poison. So, be safe rather than sorry and haul your boy off to the veterinarian.

8 **I would get bored eating the same thing every day. Doesn't my Russell need variety in his diet, too?** No, your dog does not need to eat different foods every day. In fact, his intestinal good health depends on his having a consistent diet. When you change his diet, he will experience intestinal distress. However, there are certain medical conditions that may require your dog to be on a different diet at some point in his life. Your veterinarian will make recommendations for any changes in your pet's diet.

9 **My Russell is drinking a lot more water than usual. Does that mean he's sick?** If your dog has been exercising or exposed to hot temperatures, he will consume more water. On hot summer days, it's not unusual for a dog to drink more water than usual, for example. However, if your Russell just starts drinking excessive amounts of water for no apparent reason, you should call your veterinarian immediately.

10 **How can I tell if my Russell is overweight?** If you observe your Russell's body from his head, down his back to his rear quarters, his overall shape should resemble an hourglass, tapering slightly just behind the rib cage. Another test is to place your hands, palms down, with thumbs touching, across the middle of his back. Now fan the fingers of each hand around the rib cage. If you can feel the outline of his ribs, then his weight is good. If you have to press hard to feel his ribs, he's probably overweight. There should be only a thin layer of fat covering his ribs. On the other hand, if his ribs protrude, he's underweight.

Chapter Seven

Training and Activities

The Russell is a breed that above all needs to have something positive to do. He needs to be challenged both mentally and physically to be happy and to fulfill his natural instincts as a working breed. What better and more productive way to accomplish this than by training him to obey? Training will be one of the most challenging activities you and your Russell embark on together. Having a well-trained dog is one of the true joys of pet ownership, because it says that you and your Russell have bonded and have learned to live and work together as a team. In short, is says you respect each other and are best friends—and what can be better than that? Remember, positive training is fun for your dog.

Animals living together in the wild are quick to establish a pecking order where one is the pack leader and the others fall in line behind. This behavior has been documented in many species of animals, in packs of wolves in particular. Knowing one's place in the pack takes the stress out of daily life because each member of the pack knows what's expected of him. Dogs are pack animals. A puppy's littermates make up his first pack where he is used to having a specific place in the hierarchy. Dogs function best when they understand where they belong in the general scheme of things. Thus, training begins when you first bring your puppy home. From his point of view, his new human family is replacing his littermates and becomes his new pack. Pack leadership must be established immediately or the puppy will become confused and frustrated. He wants you to assume the leadership role. But if you do not, your Russell is intelligent enough to challenge you for authority. This leads to increasing discipline problems as your dog matures. Avoid this pitfall by starting his education early with some basic training commands. You'll find your Russell is a willing student and a quick learner, once he knows his boundaries. Remember, a little patience, trust, and consistency will take you a long way on the journey toward a great relationship with your dog.

There are many schools of training and practically as many training methods. But whatever method you choose to use with your Russell, establishing yourself as the pack leader is essential. You can be an active (alpha) leader or

FYI: Choke and Slip Collars

Despite its name, a choke collar is not meant to "choke" the dog, but should be used only for mild correction. Choke and slip collars function similarly, except the slip collar is made of fabric, i.e., nylon or leather, and the choke is made of metal links with a ring on each end. The choke and slip collar allow the trainer to give the dog a quick correction by tightening when pressure is applied and then loosening immediately once the pressure has stopped. The collar must be correctly placed on the dog so that it doesn't "stick" in the tight position once pressure is released.

a passive one. An active leader responds to an action. If your dog exhibits an unwanted behavior like jumping on a bed, the active leader will correct the behavior by doing something—perhaps removing the dog from the bed and putting him in his crate. A passive leader will simply ignore the fact that the dog jumped on the bed and say nothing. The theory behind passive leadership is that animals act in order to get attention. Thus, proponents of this method believe that if the dog's behavior is ignored and doesn't result in any attention, *positive* or *negative*, the specific behavior will stop. In his book *Horses Never Lie: The Heart of Passive Leadership*, Mark Rashid talks about his experience using passive leadership with horses. Many trainers prefer a compromise: to ignore bad behavior and reward good behavior.

Before you embark on any training program, it's important to set realistic goals. Don't expect your Russell to understand what you want him to do right away. Start training a young puppy with several short, 15–30-second sessions. He won't be able to stay focused longer than that. Once he's six months old, you can increase training sessions to fifteen minutes at a time.

Before beginning a training session, have all your training tools available, i.e.: leash, choke or slip collar, and long lead. Your Russell should always be under some type of control while you are training him, whether on a leash or confined in your living room. Always make training fun for your Russell. Have a plastic baggie filled with his favorite treats and reward him each time he does what you ask him to do.

To correctly place a choke or slip collar around your Russell's neck, loop one end of the collar through the other end. Now hold the collar directly in front of you, making it form the letter *P*. Without changing the direction, slip it around your Russell's neck. In this position, the choke collar is able to release quickly after you give it a slight tug. If the *P* is in the backward position, it cannot release.

When purchasing a choke collar be sure you get the right size for your Russell. Measure his neck and then add three inches. If possible, bring your boy with you to the pet store and try the collar on. It bears repeating that choke and slip collars are *not* for everyday use and should never be left on

your pet once a training session is over or after you bring your dog in from his walk.

Training requires an infinite amount of patience and persistence, so don't give in to frustration by yelling or using a harsh tone with your boy if he doesn't get it right away. When using the choke collar and lead, never jerk the lead to make him obey. This will result in the opposite behavior and foster a negative association toward training. Learning takes time, and training sessions should always be positive so your Russell will look forward to them.

As you get ready for your first training session, keep in mind the following seven simple rules:

1. Set realistic goals—don't expect too much too soon.
2. Keep your sessions short.
3. Keep your commands simple—one-two words only.
4. Keep focused—don't introduce extraneous things into a session, such as playing with your Russell.
5. Be consistent—use the same commands in every session.
6. Be positive—praise your Russell every time he performs correctly.
7. Be patient—if he doesn't perform correctly, don't scold him; simply repeat the command. If he still doesn't get it right, end the session on an up note like taking him for a brisk walk.

It's also helpful to begin training sessions when your Russell has an empty stomach. This will make treats all the more appealing and will be an incentive for him to do as you ask.

Once you start training your puppy, consider enrolling him in puppy kindergarten. It's not only a great way to socialize him, but it will also give you the opportunity to reinforce your at-home training in a group situation that will be fun for both of you. It will also set a precedent for future activities you and your boy can enjoy together.

My Name Is . . .

What's in a name? In the case of your Russell, teaching him to respond to his name is a good way to jump-start his training in a benign and fun way. Try to have a name picked out for your dog before you bring him home. Don't let members of the household try out different names on the new puppy, because that will only serve to confuse him. It's best if everyone in the family agrees on a name beforehand; then when you bring your boy home, make sure everyone addresses him by that name and only that name. Avoid endearments like *honey, sweetie, baby, bud, boy*, and so on until your Russell learns his actual name.

The Russell is a very alert breed, so when you speak to him, he will generally look in your direction. Begin name training by simply addressing him: "Jack." When he responds by looking at you, give him a treat. Then walk to another part of the room. Call his name: "Jack." When he comes, give him a treat. Now go into another room and repeat the process until he comes to you. Then give him a treat again. Keep this up and gradually replace the treat with a pat on the head or a rub on his flanks. Soon he will associate his name with good things, namely, attention from you. Thereafter, anytime he hears you call "Jack," he'll be right there waiting for you to give him his next cue.

Helpful Hints

To get the most out of training, incorporate your Russell's natural prey drive into training sessions. At the end of a session engage him in a game of tug-of-war or reward him with a toy that resembles prey, such as a fuzzy mouse or rabbit.

Training Commands

The *Come* Command

Closely associated with name training is the next most important command: *come*. Teaching your dog to come on command can save his life. Just think about it. You're taking your boy on his regular walk. Suddenly, you stumble and inadvertently let go of the leash. Your Russell starts running ahead, and is about to run across the street. You quickly and firmly call him: *"Jack, come!"* He puts on the brakes, turns, and comes back to you. You praise him lavishly and realize that your training may have just saved him from getting lost or being hit by a car.

FYI: Enforcing Commands

Even in your early training sessions, you must be ready to enforce every command you issue to your Russell. This is important because this breed will not respect your authority unless you are ready to hold your ground. Besides training your dog, you are also establishing yourself as the pack leader. Thus, when you command him to come, he must come, even if you have to gently reel him in. He will soon learn what is expected of him and that you are serious about enforcing it. Remember, don't scold him if he doesn't obey on his own or he will have negative associations with obedience. For example, if you say, "*Jack, come*" and he doesn't move, reel him in gently and praise him: "*Good boy, Jack.*" If you scold or whack him, or drag him by the neck, in his mind he'll associate coming to you when called with being punished.

If you have a young puppy, begin your lesson by playing the "come game" with him. Sit on the floor a good distance from the puppy with a handy bag of treats. Then call him in a cheerful, happy tone: "*Jack, come!*" Clap your hands enthusiastically to get his attention. More than likely, he will bound toward you almost immediately. If not, repeat the command and the happy clapping. When he arrives, give him a treat while praising him, "Good boy!" Repeat the "come game" several times. Soon, your Russell will be bounding toward you without hesitation each time you call him. In his mind, "come" is a really fun thing to do!

As the puppy gets older or if you have an adult Russell, it's time to progress to a more formal "come" session. Begin indoors. Correctly place a choke or slip collar around his neck. Attach a lead of six feet or longer to the collar. Hold the loose end of the lead and walk away from your dog. Stop and turn to face him. Issue the command, "*Jack, come,*" and then gently reel in the lead toward you, until your dog is standing in front of you. Give him a treat and praise him. Repeat this several times until he gets the idea. It may take days or even weeks of short sessions, but hang in there.

Now it's time to kick up the exercise a notch. This time, issue the command, "*Jack, come,*" and as you do, instead of reeling him toward you, just tug slightly at the lead. If your dog comes to you on his own, give him a treat and praise him. If he doesn't, don't repeat the command, just begin to reel him in again. Keep practicing this until he comes without your having to either tug at the lead or reel him in. It will probably take several training sessions, so don't get discouraged. Just keep it fun. If you see that your boy is getting distracted or losing his focus, end the session. Remember to keep all initial training sessions short—no more than 15 minutes for an older puppy or adult. For a young puppy, sessions should be decidedly shorter.

Once your Russell has gotten the hang of the *come* command indoors, it's time to take him outside in the yard with all its myriad distractions like

birds, squirrels, the neighbors' cat, and so on, and practice your recall. This is especially important if you want your Russell to compete in obedience, agility, or earthdog trials at a later date. Your ultimate goal is to teach your Russell to come when called, without hesitation, regardless of where he is or what else may be going on around him. This will not happen overnight. It will take many weeks and even months to get your boy to the point where he will ignore everything else around him and come to you when called.

The *Sit* Command

After you bring your new Russell home, you will realize the necessity to teach him to sit as soon as possible. The Russell is so active and energetic that despite his small size he can easily knock you over as he runs relays around the house. This is especially true if there are small children in the family. He also loves to leap and twirl. Although this super-active behavior may be amusing for a time, it can get out of hand if your Russell doesn't understand when it's time for him to settle down. You can begin teaching your Russell to sit while he is mastering the *come* command.

With the long lead attached to his choke collar, command your Russell to *come*. As he comes toward you, hold a treat above his eye level. As he looks up, his rear will slope down slightly. With your free hand press down gently on his rear, and he will immediately go into a sitting position. Praise him and give him the treat. Note, you have not put a name to this command as yet, but are simply getting him used to coming when called and sitting in front of you when he does.

Once he has mastered the *come* and *sit*, you're ready to concentrate on the *sit* command by itself. What you will do now is attach a word, *sit*, to the action he already knows.

Start by placing your Russell in front of you. Hold a treat just above his eye level with your right hand. This will cause him to look up. Now give the command, *"Jack, sit"* while gently pressing down on his rear with your left hand. He already knows how to do this; what he's learning now is that this action is called *sit*. As soon as he sits, give him the treat and praise him.

The *Down* Command

Along with *come*, the *down* or *drop* command is an important one for your dog to master. Essentially, it teaches your dog to freeze and drop to the ground, no matter what he's doing. Case in point: Your Russell gets away from you and bolts after a rabbit. You yell, *"Jack, down!"* and immediately your boy stops and literally drops to the ground, just before he was about to bullet across the street into the path of an oncoming car. Can you appreciate the advantage and necessity of the well-mastered *down* command? Like the *come* command, the *down* is an absolute necessity for a Russell to master. It, too, will save his life.

Again, it cannot be stressed enough that this is a prey- and quarry-driven breed. Your Russell will take off after anything that moves. It doesn't mean that he's a bad or a stupid dog. It's simply in his nature to give chase. However, it's also in his nature to work, which means becoming part of a team with his master. Thus obedience training is a way to allow the Russell to fulfill his imperative as a working dog while also learning commands that can give his life meaning and maybe even save it someday.

Breed Truths

No matter how well you train your Russell, always keep in mind that he is a prey-driven breed and that his natural instinct can and will supersede even the best training. This does not mean that training is a useless endeavor because he will bolt anyway when he has the inclination. What it does mean is that you must be aware of the breed's propensities and take the necessary precautions. For example, when your Russell is outside of his fenced-in yard area, have him under control by keeping him on a lead. Remember, one frisky rabbit or squirrel can be a recipe for disaster for an unleashed Russell.

The *down* position is a natural one for your dog. In fact, it's the first one he learned from birth. Begin teaching your Russell the *down* command by asking him to sit. Once he is in the sitting position, kneel alongside him and hold a treat just above his eye level while you gently lay your free hand between his shoulders. Gradually lower the treat until it touches the floor. At the same time, with your other hand gently press down on your Russell's shoulder blades as you issue the command, "*Jack, down!*" Your dog should ease into a *down* position. When he does this, praise him and give him the treat. If he resists, put him into a *sit* position again. While kneeling alongside him, stretch one arm over his shoulders and with each hand, take one of his paws. Give him the command, "*Jack, down*," and as you do, gradually pull his paws out in front of him until he's down on the floor. Then praise him and give him a treat.

Since the *down* is a submissive posture for a dog, your Russell may initially resist being asked to assume this position. Thus, it may take a bit more patience and focus to master the *down*, but it is time well spent, so don't give up!

Helpful Hints

When training your Russell, it's a good practice to use hand signals as well as verbal commands. As your pet ages, he may lose some or all of his hearing, so if he's used to communicating through hand signals, he won't feel isolated and you won't become frustrated because he can't hear you.

The *Stay* Command

Like the *come* and *down* commands, the *stay* command is an invaluable tool to keep your Russell under control and out of harm's way. However, *stay* may be the hardest command for a Russell to master, not because he doesn't get it, but because he is so full of energy that "staying" in one position is just not something his brain wants to compute. But once he has mastered the other commands, the *stay* is like the icing on the cake—it just makes the whole package all the sweeter. By the time you have advanced to the *stay* command, you and your Russell are already functioning as a team. Your boy is having fun learning new things, and he is looking to you for cues to keep adding to his body of knowledge.

Teach your Russell to stay by having him sit in front of you. Hold up your hand in a "stop" position. As you do, give the command, "*Jack, stay.*" Then slowly walk a few steps away from him, turn, and face him. Do not look him in the eyes. If he's still in a sitting position, count silently to ten and then call him, "*Jack, come!*" If he comes, praise him and give him a treat. If he does not stay as commanded, just return him to the starting position and repeat the exercise. You'll have to do this several times before he understands what you want. Once he begins to stay on command, increase the time until you call him. Aim for ten seconds to start. Then increase it gradually: twenty, thirty seconds, one minute, five minutes, and so on. Finally, add some distraction. Walk around your dog, to the side of him, and so on.

The longer you are able to keep your boy in a *stay*, the better you are functioning as team. If you decide to pursue an obedience title with your Russell, the long *down-stay* is mandatory.

Leash Training

Who hasn't observed the familiar scene of a frustrated owner gripping a leash with both hands as his dog literally pulls him down the street like a sled in the Iditarod? The Russell is a small dog, but if he is not trained to walk on a leash properly, he will tug, pull, and lunge every time you take him out. Instead of looking forward to your walks together, you'll come to dread them. Walking your dog should be a pleasant experience for you and your pet. To accomplish this, you must train your Russell to walk with you, not away from you. Most dogs initially resist being walked on a leash. You'll have to gradually acclimate your puppy to the experience. Start by attaching a light puppy leash of about four feet in length to your boy's collar. Let him drag it around for a while to get used to it. Then gently pick up the loose end and walk with him. After he gets used to the leash, step up his training by guiding him to walk with you. At first he'll be all over the place, so call him over in an enthusiastic, happy tone. If he comes, praise him. If he doesn't, coax him toward you again in a happy voice. When he comes, praise him. Repeat this exercise for the first few training sessions until he shows no resistance to walking with you on his leash.

Learning to Heel

The ultimate objective of leash training is to get your dog to walk alongside you and be responsive to your movements. The *heel* command means exactly what it says: It teaches your Russell to stay close to your heels. In other words, when you are walking together, he must stay closely at your left side. When you stop, he stops. When you resume walking, he resumes with you.

Start the lesson by attaching a six-foot soft lead (either nylon or narrow leather) to his choke or slip collar. Stand him on your left side. Hold a small length of the leash in lightly your left hand. With your right hand, hold the end of the leash securely. With your left foot, take a step forward while simultaneously giving the command, "*Jack, heel*." If he doesn't move, a slight tug on the leash with your left hand will cue him. When he starts to move, praise him and continue to walk forward. Do not allow him to walk in front of you. The object of this exercise is to keep him at your left side. His neck should be even with your leg. If he pulls ahead, stop and begin the exercise again. Do not jerk the leash to pull him back if he races ahead. The repetition of the exercise along with a gentle tug on the leash as you repeat the *heel* command is all that's necessary for him to understand. Once he is heeling without much prompting, you can start to pick up your pace: Walk more briskly, do circles, change directions, make it a game—anything to challenge your Russell. You'll be surprised how much fun he will have!

Next, add the *sit* position to the exercise. Begin walking, heeling your dog, then stop. With your left hand, gently press down on his rear until he sits. Praise him, then begin walking again, stop, make him sit, and start over. Soon you will notice that his attention is totally focused on you as he begins to heel and sit simply by watching your actions.

After all training sessions, always remove the choke or slip collar and replace it with your Russell's everyday buckle or snap collar. A choke collar can easily become looped onto a hook,

Breed Truths

Teaching your Russell to master the heel command is one of the best things you can do for him, because it trains him to be totally cued in to your movements. He must be absolutely focused on you in this exercise. For a Russell, exercises of this nature that require him to use his brain give him an increased sense of purpose, which fulfills his breed need as a working terrier. Remember, the terrier of old had to be focused on his job, which was to flush quarry for his master. This gave him a sense of purpose and contentment. Today's terrier may never have the experience of the hunt, but he can still work alongside his master by learning new skills. That's why obedience training in all its myriad forms is so well suited to the Russell. Even if he resists at first, once he knows what he's supposed to do, he'll enjoy each new command you teach him.

stuck between or underneath closed doors, or inadvertently become attached to other household items and literally choke your dog. If you walk your Russell with a choke collar, use it in addition to his regular collar, which should contain his ID information. Then remove just the choke collar after the walk.

Trials and Activities

There are many activities and events geared toward furthering the function of working dogs like the Russell. The AKC sponsors many specialized competitive activities and also supports individual clubs that sponsor them. If you decide to compete in events that engage your Russell's natural abilities as a working terrier, it will take training and preparation to develop your boy's mental and physical strength, courage and reliability.

Breed Truths

Working toward an obedience, utility, agility, or earthdog title with your Russell is not only a great outlet to continue his socialization, but a fun way for you and your boy to enjoy activities together, which essentially fulfills his need to be a productive working dog. It's also a great way for you to strengthen the bond with your pet.

A good place to start is with puppy kindergarten, where he will learn from an early age to mingle with other dogs without being snappy or aggressive. It is essential for your Russell to learn to work as a member of a team early on. It will make him responsive and cooperative when you enter him into trials like obedience, agility, or go-to-ground. These are all grueling competitions that require a dog that is not only physically strong, but who also has a hardy spirit, and a willingness and singleness of purpose to do the appointed task. You can't just show up at an event and expect your dog to perform well or at all if he has never worked as part of a team.

This type of preparation goes well beyond simple obedience training. You must be dedicated to working with your Russell and taking him to training classes as he learns to fulfill his breed imperative as a working terrier. Training for either agility or utility is a far more rigorous task than simple conformation training. However, if you embark on this path with your Russell, you can be satisfied with the knowledge that you are truly raising your boy to do what he was bred to do, and you'll both have a sense of enormous accomplishment and lost of fun along the way!

The AKC sponsors a variety of shows and trials that your AKC-registered Russell is eligible to enter. Rules and regulations for each type of event are available on the official AKC website: *www.akc.org*.

Canine Good Citizen

One of the best ways to get your Russell ready to compete in shows, trials, and other fun activities is for him to earn a Canine Good Citizen (CGC) certificate. The AKC established a Canine Good Citizen program in 1989. Basically, it is designed to reward dogs who have good manners at home and in the community. The CGC is a ten-step test that lays the foundation for other activities like obedience, agility, and other performance events. Teaching CGC skills is also a good way to build your Russell's confidence and get him used to the training process.

In order to get his CGC certificate, your Russell must pass all of the following tests:

Test 1: Accept a friendly stranger
Test 2: Sit politely while being petted
Test 3: Be well groomed
Test 4: Walk on a loose (20-foot) lead
Test 5: Walk through a crowd
Test 6: Sit and go down on command and a long stay
Test 7: Come when called
Test 8: Reaction to another dog
Test 9: Reaction to distraction
Test 10: Supervised separation

The evaluator supplies a 20-foot lead for the test. The owner/handler brings the dog's brush or comb to the test.

Since its inception, the Canine Good Citizen Program has had an extremely positive effect in many communities across the country and throughout the world. Furthermore, it ensures that the dogs we cherish will always be welcomed and well-respected members of our communities.

SQUEEZE ME

Obedience Trials

The American Kennel Club held the first obedience trials in the 1930s. The purpose of the competition is to test the dog's ability to obey a set of commands while performing a set of tasks in three levels or classes of increasing difficulty.

There are three levels of competition in obedience:

I. NOVICE—designed for the dog just getting started in obedience. Exercises include the following:

- Heel on Leash and Figure Eight—demonstrates how well the dog has learned to watch his owner/handler and adjust his pace to stay with the owner/handler.
- Heel Free—performed off leash.
- Stand for Examination—demonstrates the dog's willingness to allow a "go-over" by the owner/handler, a judge, a veterinarian, etc.
- Recall—demonstrates the dog's immediate response whenever called by his owner/handler.
- Long Sit (1 minute)—demonstrates the dog's willingness to allow his owner/handler control.
- Long Down (3 minutes)—demonstrates the dog's willingness to remain in a *down* position.

II. OPEN—this level includes more complicated exercises that teach the dog to do a variety of tasks while following either voice or signal commands. Exercises include the following:

- Heel Free and Figure Eight—Same as Novice, but off leash.
- Drop on Recall—a lifesaving command for your Russell, since it gives the owner/handler control in any potentially dangerous situation.
- Retrieve on Flat
- Retrieve Over High Jump
- Broad Jump
- Long Sit (3 minutes)—similar to the long sit in Novice, but the position must be held for a longer period of time with the owner/handler out of the dog's sight.
- Long Down (5 minutes)—dog must remain in a *down* position.

III. UTILITY—This is the highest level of obedience competition. Exercises include the following:

- Signal Exercise—demonstrates the dog's ability to understand and correctly respond to the owner/handler's signal to *stand, stay, down, sit,* and *come.* No voice commands are allowed; only hand signals are given.
- Scent Discrimination—demonstrates the dog's ability to find the owner/handler's scent among a pile of articles.
- Directed Retrieve—demonstrates the dog's ability to follow a directional signal to retrieve a glove and promptly return it to the owner/handler.
- Moving Stand and Examination—the dog must *heel, stand,* and *stay* as the owner/handler moves away from him. The dog must stay and accept an examination by the judge and return to the owner/handler on command.
- Directed Jumping—the dog must go away from his owner/handler, turn, and *sit.* Then, the dog must clear whichever jump his owner/handler indicates and immediately return to the owner/handler.

There are five obedience titles awarded to a dog who has successfully completed a class: CD (Companion Dog), awarded to a dog in the Novice class; CDX (Companion Dog Excellent) awarded to a dog in the Open class; UD (Utility Dog) awarded to a dog in the Utility class; UDX (Utility Dog Excellent) to a dog who has received qualifying scores in both Open B and Utility B at 10 separate licensed or member obedience trials; and OTCH (Obedience Trial Championship), the highest obedience title a dog can win.

Any of the above titles awarded are then added after your dog's AKC-registered name and become a part of his permanent title. The jewel in the crown is the NOC (National Obedience Champion) title. This prestigious title is awarded annually to one dog who wins the AKC National Obedience Invitational. The letters *NOC* are placed before the dog's AKC-registered name and become part of the dog's permanent title.

AKC Obedience titles can be earned only at an AKC-licensed or member club trial. The Novice (CD) title must be completed before an exhibitor can enter the Open class. The Open title (CDX) must be earned before an exhibitor can enter the Utility class.

Agility Trials

Agility trials began in England in 1978. The AKC held its first agility trial in 1994. It is one of the fastest-growing and most popular dog sports in the United States. Agility is a fun way for you and your Russell to work together navigating a variety of obstacle courses consisting of things like tires, tunnels, mazes, A-frames, seesaws, and so on, racing against the clock. But make no mistake: An agility trial is an athletic event that requires your dog (and you) to be in top physical condition. He also must be exceptionally well trained, singularly focused on the task at hand, and work with you as a teammate. The AKC offers three types of agility classes, each with increasing levels of difficulty to earn the titles of Novice, Open, Excellent, and Master.

Earthdog Trials

Earthdog or "go-to-ground" trials are probably the most fun for a Russell, which is hardly surprising considering he gets to do what he was bred to do: locate quarry. In AKC and other earth events, the goal is to simulate a real hunting environment, except that neither the dog nor the quarry gets hurt. The dog enters a tunnel and must find the quarry (caged rats) at the end, signaled by barking, digging, and whining. The AKC has developed three levels of Earthdog tests: Junior Earthdog, Senior Earthdog, and Master Earthdog. The level of competition determines the difficulty of the tunnel, i.e., the number of turns involved. The dog that locates the prey in the fastest time is considered the winner.

Helpful Hints

To prepare your Russell for agility or earth trials, take it slowly. Wait until your puppy is fully developed and his concentration is focused. Spend time each day building his cardiovascular strength. Make sure his weight is good. Then gradually introduce some obstacles like small jumps into his daily play. If you make it fun, he'll soon master these initial challenges, his confidence will grow, and he'll be better prepared to step up to the next level of training.

The American Working Terrier Association (AWTA) also sponsors earthwork and above-ground events. Founded in 1971, its mission is to encourage breeders to retain the hunting instincts in their lines by breeding terriers of correct size and disposition to perform as working dogs.

The AWTA holds field trials throughout the country all year long. It issues the following certificates: certificates of gameness (CG) to dogs who qualify in the Open Division at trial; certificates of hunting (CH) to dogs used regularly for hunting for at least a period of one year; and working certificates (WC) to dogs that qualify for working in a natural den. The AWTA also publishes an informative quarterly magazine, *Down to Earth*, for members, who are encouraged to submit accounts of their hunting experiences with their dogs. It also lists dates.

Conformation Shows

If you purchased a "show" rather than a "pet" puppy, you will probably want to exhibit him once you have registered him with the AKC. Also known as canine "beauty" contests, conformation shows are the signature events of the AKC. A conformation dog show measures how well your dog *conforms* to the established written standard for his breed. These shows focus on the distinctive features of purebred dogs and thereby help to preserve these characteristics by providing a forum at which to evaluate breeding stock. The standard for each recognized breed is established by their parent clubs, in this case the Parson Russell Terrier Association of America. The written standard describes the ideal size, color, and temperament for the Russell, as well as correct proportion, structure, and movement. To become an AKC champion of record, your Russell will have to be awarded a total of 15 points in conformation shows, including two majors (wins of 3, 4 or 5 points) awarded by at least three different judges. Each dog competing must be presented to a judge either by his owner or by a professional dog handler. The handler is like a jockey in a horse race, exhibiting the dog in a way that will show off his best features. Males and females compete separately within the breed. Based on your Russell's age and experience, he must be entered into one of seven classes at each conformation show to compete for his championship.

- Puppy—For dogs between 6 and 12 months of age, that are not yet champions (optional class)
- Twelve-to-Eighteen Months—For dogs 12 to 18 months of age, that are not yet champions (optional class)
- Novice—For dogs 6 months of age and over, who have not, before the date of closing of entries, won three first prizes in the Novice Class, a first prize in Bred-by-Exhibitor, American-bred, or Open Classes, nor one or more points toward their championship (optional class)
- Amateur Owner-Handler—For dogs that are at least six months of age that are not champions. Dogs must be handled in the class by the registered owner of the dog, and the class is limited to exhibitors who have not, at any point, been a professional dog handler or AKC-approved conformation judge, or employed as an assistant to a professional handler (effective January 1, 2009—optional class)
- Bred by Exhibitor—For dogs that are exhibited by their owner and breeder, that are not yet champions (optional class)
- American-Bred—For dogs born in the United States from a mating that took place in the United States, that are not yet champions (mandatory class)
- Open—For or any dog of the breed, at least six months of age (mandatory class)

A winner is selected from each of the above classes. From those winners, the judge selects the best, who becomes Winner's Dog and wins the points allocated for males in that show. Only the best male (Winner's Dog) and the best of the females (Winner's Bitch) are awarded championship points. The Winner's Dog and Winner's Bitch then compete with the champions for the Best of Breed award.

Showing Your Russell

If you're not ready to bear the expense of a professional handler, try exhibiting your Russell yourself. Although the idea may be daunting at first, especially if you've never done it before, it's a fun activity to share with your Russell, and a great way to meet new doggy friends! Most local dog clubs offer conformation classes where owners get together one or two nights a week with an instructor, who is usually a professional handler, and learn how to show their dogs. In the process, you'll build your confidence and that of your Russell and also pick up some good pointers on how to show your boy to his best advantage. In addition, most local clubs also have "matches," which are like practice shows, based on the AKC regular conformation shows. Although winners are chosen, no points are awarded. However, match shows offer the opportunity for you and your boy to test and hone your skills in the ring while having a great time.

If you decide to exhibit your Russell yourself:

- Make sure your Russell is AKC registered.
- Make sure your Russell is current on all inoculations.
- Learn proper grooming and exhibiting techniques before showing your Russell.
- Join the PRTAA or a Local Specialty and/or All-Breed club in your area.
- Become familiar with the AKC rules and regulations for dog shows.
- Attend dog shows and watch how the Russell is exhibited and judged.
- Ask your breeder for advice.
- Ask other Russell owners and exhibitors for advice.
- Enroll in handling classes with your Russell.

Hiking and Camping with Your Russell

There's no better and more willing companion for an overnight camping trip or a long hike in the woods than your Russell. His natural instinct is to explore new things. He also loves to be outdoors. Before you set off into the

natural kingdom, make sure your Russell is obedience trained. Bear in mind that that won't keep him from chasing after a fox or a rabbit if he's unleashed. Your boy is a natural hunter, and his instinct can and will supersede your commands. Thus, it is not advisable to let him run free. Even if you have scouted out an area ahead of time, allowing your Russell to chase anything that catches his eye can be detrimental to the both of you. Play it safe and enjoy the great outdoors with your Russell right by your side. Don't feel guilty and think that you're depriving him. Your Russell is really the happiest when he is spending high-quality time with his master.

Helpful Hints

Make sure to take enough water along when camping or hiking with your Russell. If it's hot, hike in the early morning or late afternoon. Avoid night hikes, but if you get caught after dark, make sure you and boy are wearing reflectors. At the end of a hike, check his coat for ticks and his feet for cuts, scratches, or foreign objects, especially if you've been on rocky terrain.

Therapy Work

There's nothing more rewarding than to watch a smile creep onto a sick child's face when an animal is brought to a hospital bedside. More and more dogs and cats are being used to visit patients in hospitals, nursing homes, and even prisons. The therapeutic effects of stroking an animal are well documented—so much so that animals are being used more frequently in hospitals and nursing homes to visit with patients. Animals are also used in therapy. Animal-Assisted Therapy (AAT) is an accepted part of some patient treatment programs. In AAT, a therapy dog and a handler are assigned to a specific patient with a set of specific goals. The handler and the health care provider consult on the goals to be accomplished, and then plan how to accomplish them using the animal. For example one patient goal might involve picking up a brush and stroking the dog for a certain number of times. The patient's progress is recorded and the treatment protocols are advanced as the patient accomplishes the goals. There are several agencies that provide this type of therapy, but you can also volunteer by checking with your community service center for programs that are available. If your Russell is well socialized and obedience trained, he is ideally suited to therapy work because he is such a fun-loving people dog. Knowing that you and your boy are making a positive difference in someone else's life is, in itself, a cause for celebration. If you'd like to know more about therapy work, there are many animal therapy websites online or you can log on to *www.dogplay.com.*

Leash Training

1 Attach a leash to your puppy's collar, and allow him to walk around with it dragging on the ground for a few moments, just to get used to it. He's a curious Russell, so don't be surprised if he starts making circles and trying to catch it!

2 Gently pick up the end of the leash and follow in the direction your puppy takes you. If he suddenly stops, drop the end of the leash and let him drag it again. Then quietly pick up the end and follow his lead. He'll soon get used to having you on the other end of the leash.

3 Get your puppy to follow you by holding out a treat and coaxing him over. When he moves toward you, give him the treat. If he starts to go in a different direction, lure him back again with another treat.

4 Keep coaxing your puppy to follow you for greater distances. Do not jerk on the leash. Instead, use an encouraging tone of voice and a treat to lure him. Gradually you will be able to withdraw the treat and substitute praise as he begins walking happily by your side. If he pulls ahead on the leash, coax him back to your side with a treat, then praise him and continue walking together.

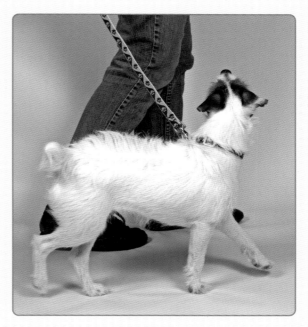

The *Sit* Command

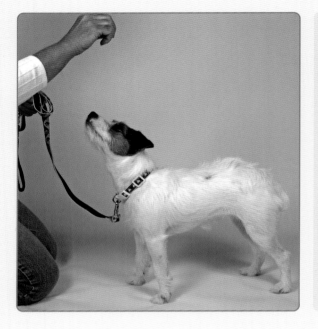

1 With your Russell standing, take out a treat and slowly bring it up just above the level of his eyes. As his head tilts upward, with your free hand, press lightly on his rear quarters and give the command, "*Sit.*" If he sits, say "Good!" and give him the treat. Practice this several times, rewarding him each time he sits.

2 Stand your Russell, take out a treat, and slowly bring it just above his eye level. As his head tilts upward, give the command, "*Sit.*" If he sits without you pressing on his rear quarters, say "Good" and reward him with the treat. If he does not, gently press on his rear, and when he sits, give him the treat. Then say "Good" and try it again until he sits on his own, without having to press on his rear. Be sure to tell him he's good, and give him the treat every time he sits.

3 Stand your Russell, and point your finger, drawing an imaginary line from his nose to above his head with a sweeping motion. His eyes will probably follow your finger, his head automatically tilting upward, which will make his rear start to slope down. Now give the command, "*Sit*." If he sits, give him a treat from your other hand and praise him.

4 Gradually abbreviate your hand movement until you are using only a small hand signal along with the verbal signal, "*Sit!*" Keep practicing and rewarding/praising him each time he gets it right.

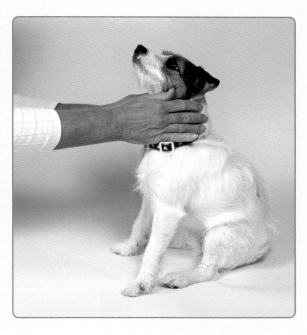

The *Stay* Command

1 Have your Russell sit; then say "*Stay*" while holding your palm in a "stop" signal in front of his face. If he gets up, don't scold him; simply put him back in position and start over. A puppy has a short attention span, so it will take quite a few times for him to understand what's expected.

2 With your Russell leashed, put him into a sitting position in front of you and give him the *stay* command. While holding the end of the leash, walk backward several steps. If he gets up to follow you, pick him up and return him to the start position and begin again. If he stays, wait for a few seconds, then release him by saying "*OK!*"

3 With your Russell leashed, put him into a sitting position and give him the *stay* command. Drop the end of the leash, walk several steps away, then turn to face him. If he gets up and comes toward you, begin again by returning to the start position. Once he has held the *stay* for several seconds, release him. Gradually increase the duration of the *stay*.

4 Put your leashed Russell into a sitting position, and give him the *stay* command. Drop the end of the leash and introduce mild distractions by moving around him. If he attempts to follow you, return him to the starting position, give him the *stay* command, and begin again. Gradually increase the duration and the distraction level until he stays reliably and you verbally release him. Remember to always praise your dog for a task well done.

143

Chapter Eight

Grooming

There is nothing more pleasing to the eye than a clean, well-groomed Russell. Just remember what your mother said: "Cleanliness is next to godliness!" The more active your Russell, the more you will appreciate this old adage. It's a fact of nature: A normal, healthy Russell is more likely than not to come into the house from play needing a good brushing or hosing down. It's just part of young Jack's charm. When he's out in the yard, he's in his element: running, frolicking, rolling around, digging, and investigating, and that could make for one messy pup by the end of the day.

Don't think that just because he's a short-coated dog, he doesn't require regular grooming. Even if your Russell doesn't crave daily mud rolls, he's bound to pick up burrs, and other vegetation when he's outdoors. Furthermore, the Russell is a shedding breed. So, if you don't want to see tenacious little white hairs all over your carpets and furniture, get into the habit of giving him a good brushing or combing before he turns in for the night.

Russells come in two coat types, smooth and broken or rough, which can be distinguished as follows: The smooth coat is short and lies flat along his body; the broken or rough coat has a smooth undercoat with longer, wiry guard hairs lying on top. Typically the rough coat gives the Russell his signature scruffy look. Although both of these coats shed, many owners swear that their smooth-coated Russells shed the most.

Breed Needs

Being a curious and high-spirited Russell isn't easy, but somebody's got to do it! If he comes in from the yard smelling like he's been on intimate terms with a skunk, do not dunk him in a vat of tomato juice. It won't do the trick. Instead head for your pet or feed store and buy a commercial de-skunking solution. Also never use turpentine, paint thinner, or kerosene on your Russell to remove yucky things like tar, paint, or sap. Instead, use petroleum jelly followed by a bath.

CHECKLIST

Grooming Supplies You'll Need

Before you prepare to groom your Russell from head to toe, have all the following supplies handy for each phase of the process:

- ✔ Tub (yours or a doggy tub)
- ✔ Natural sponge
- ✔ Cotton balls
- ✔ Washcloth
- ✔ Bath-sized terry cloth towels
- ✔ Handheld shower head
- ✔ Mineral or baby oil
- ✔ Shampoo (hypoallergenic, botanicals are best)

- ✔ Coat conditioner (optional)
- ✔ Grooming table
- ✔ Natural bristle or nylon brush
- ✔ Slicker brush
- ✔ Wide-tooth metal comb
- ✔ Stripping knife or Furminator
- ✔ Scissors
- ✔ Blunt-edged scissors
- ✔ Toenail clippers
- ✔ Kwick stop or similar styptic powder
- ✔ Doggy toothpaste
- ✔ Doggy toothbrush
- ✔ Ear cleaner

Most dogs initially resist any kind of grooming, particularly if they've never been groomed or if it's been an unpleasant experience in the past. Word to the wise? Start early on. In fact, as soon as you bring your Russell puppy home, get him used to being handled; that includes handling his feet, head, and muzzle. Begin accustoming him to regular, short grooming sessions and make them a fun experience by giving him a treat or making the grooming time a prelude to playtime, so he will look forward to it.

Regular grooming for your Russell should include bathing him, cleaning his eyes and ears, brushing his teeth, and trimming his toenails. Make daily brushing and combing part of his regular routine. Reward him after each session and he'll look forward to it. If your Russell is a working terrier, regularly takes part in terrier trials, or simply engages in rough play outside, he will need more intensive daily grooming.

Once you have all of your supplies, you're ready to get down and serious about making your boy put his best terrier foot forward. The first step is a good brushing.

Helpful Hints

When stripping your Russell, the stripping knife should be held parallel to his body to avoid a choppy look in the coat. Grasp the knife in your right hand. Take a few hairs between your thumb and the knife blade, then give a sharp pull. Until your boy becomes accustomed to stripping, do only a small area each time. To prevent him from getting bored or fidgety, have some tasty treats available, which should keep him interested and cooperative.

How to Brush Your Russell

Get your Russell started on his grooming routine by getting him used to being brushed. Brushing is an important first step because it's the best way to remove dead hair from his coat and any dirt or debris that he picks up outside. It will also give his coat a healthy gloss by stimulating the natural oils in his skin. Brushing also feels good, so it's a great way to get your boy used to being groomed.

You can brush his back, chest, sides, legs, and ears. Do not brush around the face or eye area. Instead use a moist washcloth for these delicate areas. Depending on his coat, you'll need different tools to brush him effectively.

For smooth coats, use a firm, natural bristle brush. After brushing him down, go over the area with a metal comb to catch any stray hairs.

For broken/rough coats, use a slicker brush to remove excess hair, dirt, and debris that gets nestled. Then go over him with a stripping tool to give him a nice, finished look and remove any excess hair. When your "strip" your boy's coat, you are removing the dead hair so a new wire coat can grown in. A stripping knife is used instead of a clipper because unlike the clipper, it doesn't "cut" hair but "pulls" it out by gripping the hair, thus maintaining the proper wire texture. It does not hurt the dog. Wire hair is not attached in the same way flat hair is. Most dogs enjoy being stripped once they get used to it.

The Furminator is a great patented de-shedding tool that can be used on both coat types. It quickly removes loose, dead hair without damaging the dog's topcoat.

Bathing

Unless your Russell is a working terrier, hitting the show or terrier trial circuit, you probably won't need to bathe him more than every month or two. In hot weather, you may need to bathe him more frequently. Don't overdo it, though. Excessive bathing can dry out his skin, make him shed more, and cause his coat to look dull. Allow a little common sense and a good nose to dictate his bath schedule.

CAUTION

If your Russell has a broken coat, do not use an oil-based shampoo or conditioner, as it will change the coat's natural harsh texture.

You can bathe your Russell in your bathtub or in a special doggy bathtub that you can purchase at any pet store or in pet catalogs. Even though your Russell has a natural affinity to water, he will probably resist his first dunk in the bathtub, so try to make it a fun experience by making it seem like playtime. Place some waterproof toys in the tub and initiate gentle play as you gradually wet him down. It's best to use a natural sponge or a handheld shower device. Don't pour a pail of water over him or he will become frightened. You'll soon see that he'll become so involved in playing with his toys that he won't even realize he's being bathed.

Once he's wet, use a sponge to soap him thoroughly with a mild hypoallergenic pet shampoo. Avoid getting soap into his eyes and ears. Many shampoos are "tearless," meaning that they will not irritate the eyes. Rinse him thoroughly using a handheld showerhead. Make sure you get all the soap out. You can use a coat conditioner after rinsing. Some are leave-in conditioners and others are the rinse-out type. It's best to use the rinse-out type unless you are showing your dog and want a more intensive conditioning treatment. After rinsing, towel-dry him with a plush terry cloth bath towel. Be sure to dry between his toes. Once he's used to his bathing routine, your Russell will appreciate a vigorous towel drying. Remember to remove the cotton balls from his ears and gently pat the inside of his ear flaps dry as well. Then use a warm, wet washcloth (without shampoo) to clean his face and the area around his eyes. Hair dryers are not recommended, as they tend to dry out the coat and most dogs are frightened by the sound and sensation of a dryer. However, if you must

Helpful Hints

Before bathing your Russell, place a cotton ball loosely in each ear, to keep water from getting into the ear canal, and always give his coat a good brushing and plucking to loosen any dead hair.

have him dry right away (e.g., you're on your way into the show ring), use the lowest setting on the hair dryer; otherwise your broken or rough-coated boy will have an undesirable attack of the frizzies!

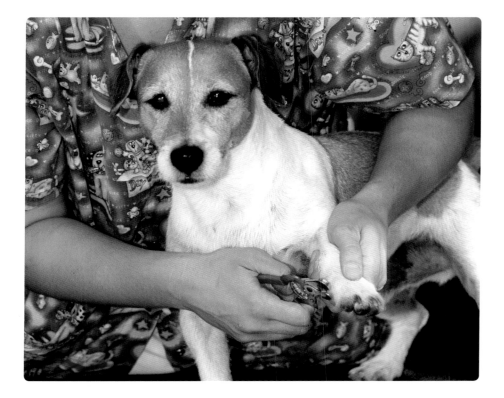

Nail Trimming

It's important to keep your Russell's nails cut. If they are too long, it will make him uncomfortable when he walks, and if you have hardwood floors, you won't appreciate the scratch marks untrimmed nails will make. If you hear a tapping sound when your Russell walks on your wood or tile floors, that means his nails need a trim. Generally, a dog's nails need to be cut every three to four weeks. However, if your Russell walks on hard surfaces like sidewalks and concrete, he may not need his nails cut as frequently.

As with all grooming, you should get your Russell used to having his nails trimmed from puppyhood; otherwise he will be resistant. Be very gentle with him and make it a pleasant experience. Remember to trim only a little of his nail at a time so you won't hurt him. That way he will not fear having a pedicure in the future.

To clip your Russell's nails you'll need:

1. a nail clipper, which you can purchase in a pet store or in a pet catalog. They come in two types: the pliers and guillotine styles. Both get the job done, so choose the one you are most comfortable using, and select a small size. Do not use a human nail clipper on your dog.

2. Kwick stop or other styptic powder or gel—just in case you cut the nail back too short, this will stop the bleeding immediately. Both are available at your pet store.

Begin trimming your Russell's nail a little bit at a time. After each cut look at the inside of the nail. If you see a pinkish color, stop. You are close to the quick, the blood vessel inside the nail. If your Russell has light-colored nails, it's fairly easy to see the quick, which looks like a pink line that runs up the nail almost to the end. On dark-colored nails, you need to look on the inside of the nail as you cut to see the quick. If you do cut the quick, immediately dip the nail into the styptic powder or gel and the bleeding will stop.

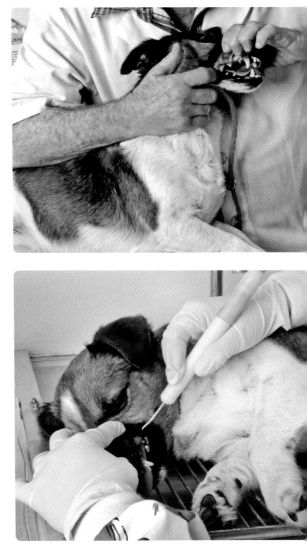

Dental Hygiene

Every grooming session, whether regular maintenance or for show, should include brushing your Russell's teeth. In fact, you should get into the habit of brushing them daily. Use a doggy toothbrush or a finger brush that fits over your index finger, and doggy toothpaste. Remember, never use human toothpaste when brushing your Russell's teeth. Rub the brush in a circular motion over your dog's teeth and gums. Don't rub too hard or he will resist. After you finish brushing, examine his mouth for any chipped or broken teeth, gum inflammation, or plaque buildup. If you see any of those things, schedule a dental checkup with the veterinarian.

Cleaning the Ears and Eyes

Because your Russell is outside quite a bit, he'll likely get into brush and other vegetation. If his ears appear healthy, it's still a good idea to clean them once a month. You can buy a mild non-alcohol-based or herbal dog ear cleaner at a pet store or from your veterinarian. You can also make up your own cleanser consisting of equal parts water and white vinegar. To clean his ears, squirt a small amount of the solution into his ear canal and massage the ear gently, in a downward motion toward the base of the ear. The dog will usually shake his head after this, which loosens any dirt or wax buildup inside the ear canal. Take a cotton ball and clean any visible dirt inside the ear flap. Never insert a cotton swab or any instrument into your dog's ear canal, as you may rupture his eardrum.

Clean your Russell's eyes with a moist cloth. If he has any discharge coming from the corners of his eyes, wipe it away. If you notice excessive discharge coming from his eyes, or if it is green or yellow, consult your veterinarian. Check the whites of his eyes by gently petting him on the head and raising his eyebrow. If you notice redness, he may have an infection or irritation and will need to see the veterinarian.

Helpful Hints

Before expressing your Russell's anal glands, make sure you hold a paper towel close to his anus to catch any fluid. Otherwise it could spray all over you—*yuk!*

Anal Gland Care

The anal glands, also dubbed the "skunk glands," are two round sacs at each side of the anus at the four and eight o'clock positions. True to their name, they expel a foul-smelling secretion, which in the male is used to mark territory. Every time a dog defecates, he normally expels anal secretion. But sometimes, dogs have difficulty expressing their anal glands, and as a result, they can become impacted. This can lead to a bacterial infection or even an abscess. If you notice that your Russell is licking his anal area excessively or scooting his rear along the floor, his glands may need expressing. It's best to take your Russell to the veterinarian to have this done. Although it is a very simple procedure, it isn't very pleasant. But if you want to learn how to do it, ask your veterinarian for a demonstration. Occasionally, a dog will need to have his anal glands removed if they develop a chronic impaction problem.

Grooming Your Russell for the Show Ring

If you selected a show puppy when you bought your Russell, it was with the intention of getting him ready to compete in conformation dog shows. Although puppies can't compete in the puppy classes until they are six months old, you'll need to start getting your future superstar ready for his big debut as soon as you bring him home.

The Russell is one of the few remaining breeds that is shown in a manner consistent with his breed function. According to the AKC standard, "the terrier is shown in his natural appearance not excessively groomed…important to breed type is a natural appearance: harsh, weatherproof coat with a compact construction and clean silhouette." His appearance and general presentation in the show ring should best exhibit his coat and structure as a working terrier. Preparing your boy for the show ring in such a way that will accentuate his good points and minimize his faults is nothing short of an art. If you've never groomed and exhibited a Russell before, ask for help from your breeder or a grooming professional who is knowledgeable about the breed. It's money well spent to have him groomed professionally the first time you show him. You can learn a lot just from watching the grooming process, and that way, you'll feel more confident before attempting it yourself.

Helpful Hints

Whether you're grooming for regular maintenance or show, take several breaks and split up the sessions the first few times you groom your Russell. This will make it easier for him to become acclimated to the process and prevent boredom. Grooming is not only one of the best ways to bond with your dog but is also an excellent form of discipline training, so have fun with it!

Once you are ready, begin grooming your Russell by standing him securely on a grooming table and slipping the safety loop collar hanging from the upright arm of the table around his neck. This will keep him from moving while you groom. Be sure the loop is not tight around his neck. Once he is secure and comfortable, use a stripping knife and begin hand stripping him from the base of the neck down the length of his body, sides, and legs in short strokes. This removes dead and loose hair. Your goal is to make your boy look neat, clean, and defined, not bald, so don't over-strip. When you can see his fine white undercoat, stop.

Next, go to his neck. Hold his skin taut as you strip. Start at the back of the neck, working your way around to the front. Then proceed to his head. Remember to use short strokes and talk to your boy as you groom. This will keep him relaxed and involved. After you strip his head, proceed to the chest area. Don't forget to strip the backs of his legs, too, so that the lines of the *stifle* or knee are visible.

Once your Russell is stripped, take the scissors and go to his feet. Most dogs hate this, so you might have to do one paw and then come back to the next one. Using the scissors, gently trim the hair between his toes so that you can clearly see his feet. Then check his anal area. Often dirt and fecal matter get trapped there, so you'll want to check regularly to keep the area clean. You also may need to trim the hairs. For this, use the blunt-tipped scissors. Finally, check his tail. If it seems bushy, use the stripper. Then trim the long hair at the tip of the tail by holding the tail firmly and cutting across with the scissors to make it even and tidy.

Now stand back and take a good look. Congratulations: Your boy is show ready!

Chapter Nine

The Senior Parson Russell Terrier

It's hard to imagine that the impish ball of energy you welcomed into your home as a puppy so many years ago could ever grow old. If any breed is analogous to James Barrie's immortal Peter Pan, it's the Russell, because like Peter this boy just doesn't want to grow up—ever! And in many ways, he never does. Nonetheless, one day when you see him moving a bit more gingerly as you pick up his lead, signaling the morning walk, or when you toss his favorite ball in the yard and he hesitates a moment before running to retrieve it, and even then runs oh, so much more carefully, you'll know something is changing. As you look into his eyes, you may notice a cloudy film covering those once deep brown orbs. And you'll probably see some white hairs insinuating themselves around his muzzle. Then you'll make a quick mental calculation and realize probably for the first time that your beloved Russell isn't a puppy anymore, he's a senior citizen! Of course, that doesn't mean he's ready to throw in the proverbial towel and spend his golden years curled up on a couch. In most cases, if your Russell has had good health care and proper nutrition throughout his life, he can look forward to a fairly active senior canine life.

You can help make your Russell's golden years happy, healthy, and productive by monitoring him for any changes and then discussing them with your veterinarian.

- ✔ Food consumption. Is he eating more, less? Does he seem to prefer soft food to kibble? Does he have difficulty chewing or swallowing? Does he vomit after eating?
- ✔ Water consumption. Is he drinking more or less than usual?
- ✔ Weight. Is he gaining or losing weight?
- ✔ Activity level. Is he having difficulty climbing stairs, getting up or down? Does he stop for a rest during walks? Does he bump into things?
- ✔ Respiration. Does he pant more than usual, especially during a walk? Does he sneeze or cough?

PERSONALITY POINTERS
Behavioral Changes in Your Senior Russell

Sign	Possible Cause
Slowness	Arthritis, heart problems, hypothyroidism
Difficulty getting up and down	Arthritis is the most common culprit in dogs as they age, and can occur in any joint but usually in the legs and spine.
Barking, whining	A Russell is a very vocal dog, but as he ages, stress caused by any changes in daily routine can trigger increased vocalization. If your senior Russell has trouble moving, he may be calling to get your attention. Whining can also signal that your dog is in pain.
Anxiety, nervousness	Older dogs become anxious and nervous when their daily routine changes, when they are left alone, or if they develop a physical problem like hearing or vision loss.
Incontinence or frequent accidents	It's common for senior dogs to "dribble" or lose some degree of bladder control. Infection, prostate problems (in a male), or kidney dysfunction can also be the culprit.
Aggression	Your Russell may be losing his vision and become startled when you approach him; he may be in pain from arthritis or other medical condition, all of which may result in his snapping or growling.
Noise phobia	Some older dogs become overly sensitive to noises because of to their inability to manage stress.
Gastrointestinal distress, constipation	Normal aging causes a slowdown in the way food moves through your Russell's digestive tract. This can result in constipation. Inactivity can also cause constipation, or it may be a sign of a more serious disease. Your dog may also have excess gas.
Senility	Normal aging, cognitive dysfunction, toxicity, brain tumor

Solution

Your veterinarian will need to make a determination about what is causing the problem and treat it accordingly. If it's just simple old age, just keep your Russell comfortable and let him set his own pace.

There are many medications and supplements to treat arthritis and lessen joint pain, but your veterinarian will have to determine if this is the problem and suggest the best treatment for your Russell.

Try to cut down on his stress level by limiting changes to his and your daily routine. If he appears to be in pain, call your veterinarian and get an advisory.

If your Russell seems to be suffering from separation anxiety, try changing your routine so he doesn't anticipate your departure. Before you leave, give him a favorite toy to keep him busy and turn on soothing music to relax him. Then quietly slip out of the house without alerting him. In extreme cases, he may need medication, so consult your veterinarian.

Take your Russell out more often so he can relieve himself. If he seems to be straining or if the problem continues, consult your veterinarian.

Schedule a visit with your veterinarian.

Identify the offending noise and try to desensitize your Russell to the sound. If he's afraid of thunder, for example, make a recording of thunder sounds and play them back to him, first at a low level, and gradually increase the volume until he's no longer bothered by it. If desensitization doesn't work, consult your veterinarian. Your dog may need medication.

Try feeding your Russell more frequent, smaller meals. Consult your veterinarian about a special diet. If constipation persists, schedule a visit with your veterinarian.

Try to stimulate your Russell by giving him favorite toys, and talking to him; if he appears to be "in a fog" or is unresponsive, schedule a visit with your veterinarian and have him evaluated.

Like most smaller breeds, a Russell can live well into his middle to late teens, and isn't generally considered a "senior" until he is about 12–13. But as he approaches old age, you will begin to notice changes in his behavior, his appearance, and his nutritional needs.

Physical Changes in the Aging Russell

One of the first things you'll notice when your Russell begins aging is white hair around his muzzle. If his muzzle is already predominately white, you'll see white hairs creeping up around the eyes and in dark hair around the face. His once shiny coat may start to lose its luster and become dull and thin. His skin also loses some elasticity and can bruise more easily than when he was younger. You may notice lesions or tumors on his skin. Although these are generally benign, they should be checked by your veterinarian.

As your Russell ages, he'll start to move a little more slowly because his joints are no longer as flexible as they once were. It's common for a Russell to become arthritic as he ages, especially if he's been a working dog. Nutritional supplements like glucosamine/chondroitin can help keep his

Helpful Hints

Dry skin is common among older dogs and can be very uncomfortable and itchy. Try giving him a daily fatty acid supplement. This will alleviate the discomfort and may even restore the luster to his coat.

joints lubricated. Your veterinarian can also proscribe medications to ease the pain and inflammation of arthritis.

Your Russell's once vaunted hearing can also become compromised as he enters his senior years. If you call to him and he doesn't respond or if he becomes startled when you approach him from behind, it's likely that he's lost some of his hearing. You may also notice that his eyes have a cloudy or bluish glaze. The medical name for this condition is *lenticular sclerosis*. It's a normal process of aging and doesn't usually affect the dog's vision. However, if you notice opaque white spots on your Russell's pupils, he could have cataracts, which can affect his vision. It's a good idea to have your Russell checked out by your veterinarian as soon as you notice signs of aging. In most cases your veterinarian will be able to recommend either treatment or medication that will make your Russell's life enjoyable and pain free as he ages.

Nutritional Needs

Your Russell's nutritional needs change during every stage in his life. Although a young, energetic puppy needs plenty of protein, the older Russell's body no longer has the same protein or caloric requirements. As his energy and activity level slows down, so too does his metabolism. That means he doesn't need as many calories as he did as a puppy or as an adult. If his diet isn't altered to reflect this change, he will become overweight and possibly even obese, which will shorten his life span considerably and make him susceptible to other diseases.

Besides cutting down on protein, fat, and calories, your older Russell will need more fiber in his diet. He will also need the appropriate balance of vitamins and minerals. If he has arthritis or other joint

Breed Needs

Just because your Russell is getting older, it doesn't mean you should stop exercising him. Even though he won't be up for the strenuous exercise he enjoyed as a young dog, he still needs to remain active. He might enjoy a less vigorous game of ball, for example. This will keep his weight down, his heart functioning well, and his mind alert. He'll also still enjoy a good walk. Maybe he won't want to go as far, but he genuinely likes to meet and greet people, and will cherish this time together with you.

problems, or a medical condition, there are prescription diets available to address most of them. Your veterinarian can advise you if your Russell needs to be on a special diet. If not, there are many good senior diets available, so do some research or ask your veterinarian for a recommendation.

Most commercial and premium dog foods have a formula available for every stage in the dog's life that contains the proper balance of nutrients to ensure his continued good health well into old age.

Common Diseases

Decreased Immune Function As your Russell ages, his immune system doesn't function as efficiently as it did when he was a youngster. This makes him more susceptible to infectious diseases, which are harder to fight off in an older dog. The best prevention is to be sure your Russell is current on all of his vaccinations.

Decreased Heart Function As your Russell ages, his heart loses its ability to pump blood throughout his body as effectively as it did when he was younger. His heart valves are no longer as elastic as they once were. If your veterinarian suspects a heart problem, he will order diagnostic tests to make a definitive diagnosis. Depending on the nature of the heart ailment, your Russell may be put on medication to control the disease.

Decreased Kidney Function Changes in kidney function are one of the by-products of old age. The older your Russell gets, the more risk he has of kidney dysfunction. The early signs of kidney problems are increased thirst and urination. Your veterinarian will have to do a blood chemistry screen and urinalysis to determine if there is loss of kidney function and the extent of deterioration. If his kidneys are not functioning normally, your Russell may have to be put on a special kidney diet (KD) and/or on medication.

Hormonal Dysfunction Hormonal problems are very common in older dogs. Some breeds, like the Russell, are at a greater risk of developing hypothyroidism, which is diagnosed through a blood test and treated with medication.

Prostate Enlargement This is a common problem in older intact male dogs. When the prostate becomes enlarged, it affects the dog's ability to urinate and defecate. Your veterinarian should check your Russell's prostate gland during regular physical exams. An enlarged prostate can also cause chronic infection called prostititis. The easy solution is to have your male Russell neutered.

Hearing Loss Some senior Russells begin to lose hearing as they age. Often the process is so gradual that you may not be aware of it until it's in an advanced stage. Some signs of hearing loss include what appears to be aggression when you touch him or walk over to him. In reality, your Russell is simply reacting instinctively because he wasn't able to hear you approaching and your touch startled him. You may also notice that he isn't obeying commands as readily as he once did because he doesn't hear them, particularly if you are calling him from another room or from a distance. For this reason, when training your Russell puppy, it's helpful to use hand signals as well as voice commands. Then if his hearing starts to wane as he gets older, you can fall back on hand signals to communicate with your boy. Although

BE PREPARED! CDS Symptoms

If your senior Russell isn't behaving like his normal self, be as specific as possible in describing your pet's symptoms. Symptoms of CDS include the following:

- Weight loss
- Appetite changes
- Confusion
- Disorientation
- Anxious look
- Staring into space
- Getting lost in the house
- Altered pattern of sleeping and waking
- Loss of learned behaviors such as obedience commands and housetraining
- Change in relationship with family such as aloofness, aggression, or inability to recognize members of the family
- Excessive vocalization such as howling, or monotonous barking

hearing loss is not generally reversible, your Russell can still sense vibrations. So you can always clap your hands or stamp your foot on the floor to get his attention.

Dental Disease

As your Russell ages, his teeth need as much attention as the rest of his body. If you've worked or hunted with your boy, his mouth needs extra attention. Have you noticed that his breath has a dang or otherwise unpleasant odor? Do his gums appear to be red or swollen? Are some of his teeth broken or missing? Does he scratch his mouth area? Is he suddenly eating less and/or refusing dog biscuits? Any or all of these signs could be an indication of periodontal disease, which is not only common in dogs but is also becoming a chronic health problem in canine seniors. When periodontal disease is left unattended, bacteria enter the bloodstream and can then lead to infection in other bodily organs. Many diseases and health problems in dogs are the direct result of neglected dental care. As your Russell ages, he is more susceptible to infection. Do him and yourself a favor by practicing good oral hygiene habits and having your veterinarian do a yearly dental checkup and cleaning.

Is Your Senior Russell Senile?

Why is your normally well-behaved Russell starting to snap for no apparent reason? Why is he suddenly having accidents in the house? Why does he stare off into space, or even worse, look right at you and seem not to know

FYI: 10 Simple Rules for Keeping Your Senior Russell Healthy

1. Keep his weight down. Obesity is one of the leading causes of health problems, particularly as your dog ages.
2. Feed him a senior dog food or a prescription diet if he has other health issues. As your Russell ages, he needs fewer calories.
3. Take him to the veterinarian for bi-yearly physical exams, which should include complete blood panel testing. Discovering a potential health problem early can make all the difference in an older pet's ability to recover.
4. Keep your Russell active. Even though his exercise level will need to be adjusted to his life stage and general health, the fit Russell is a happier and healthier dog than one who is sedentary.
5. Brush his teeth daily. Give him dental chews and a yearly dental exam at the veterinarian's office.
6. Provide him with an orthopedic dog bed. This is especially helpful if your senior Russell develops arthritis or other joint problems.
7. Keep his coat clean and well groomed.
8. Keep your Russell's nails clean and clipped. Unclipped nails can make walking very difficult, especially if your senior Russell also has arthritis and difficulty moving.
9. Keep him well socialized. Your Russell likes to be the life of the party, and that doesn't change as he gets older. He needs to be around people.
10. Give him lots of tender, loving care. It will go a long way in keeping his spirits high and his will to live strong.

who you are? These behavior changes can be very disconcerting, but they are all signs that your senior Russell is suffering from cognitive dysfunction syndrome, or CDS, also called Canine Cognitive Disorder. In layman's terms, it means your beloved old boy is becoming senile. Signs include confusion, disorientation, restlessness, especially at night, incontinence, slowness, and not recognizing family and friends. The good news is that medications are available to treat CDS. As in humans, senility is a gradual process, so much so that you may not recognize early symptoms. It involves an increasing loss of thought processes such as alertness, and the ability to learn, remember, and perceive surroundings. This condition is seen mostly in the geriatric Russell (over age 12), but it can present itself earlier. Unfortunately the behavioral changes associated with CDS can disrupt the strong bond between dog and owner. If you suspect your senior Russell is exhibiting signs of CDS, consult your veterinarian, who will give your dog a complete examination to rule out any physical illness.

Treatments

Although there is no cure for CDS, there are drugs that can effectively treat and minimize symptoms. Discuss this option with your veterinarian. The goal is to provide a better quality of life for your pet and ideally to slow the progression of the disease.

More than likely your veterinarian will want to run some tests in order to diagnose your pet's condition. Here are some of the more common tests he may need:

- Urinalysis
- Blood count
- Chemistry panel
- EKG
- Thyroid test
- X-rays

Is Your Russell's Quality of Life Declining?

No matter how vigilant you are about your Russell's health, the day will come when you pick up his leash for his daily playtime and he looks at you sadly but won't budge. All the things he used to do with such exuberance are no longer interesting to him. He simply isn't enjoying life anymore. For a Russell in particular, this isn't a situation that his brain or his heart can compute. By nature, your Russell is a fun-loving, frolicking, active, no-holds-barred ball of energy. He loves to be in high gear. He's happiest when he's at your side going about daily activities. When he can't do that any longer, he's not a happy camper, and there is nothing as sad as a Russell that has lost his zest for living. But it's probably even harder for you to admit to yourself that this is the case. The harsh reality is that our beloved pets just don't live long enough.

Saying Good-bye

If you're lucky and your beloved pet passes on from old age in his sleep one night, you'll never have to decide when the right time to say good-bye is. But for most owners, it will be the hardest and most heart-wrenching decision they've ever had to make. When your Russell becomes ill, you'll want to do all and everything you can to make him well again. Sometimes no matter how valiantly you and your veterinarian try, your pet's illness is beyond the scope of modern medicine. When your veterinarian tells you that there is nothing more to be done medically for your Russell, he may suggest that you put him to sleep and end his suffering. Some owners are not emotionally prepared to make that decision right away and wish to spend as much time as possible with their pet. As long as your dog is able to be maintained comfortably and free of pain, it is a path you may want to

consider. Nonetheless, the reality is that ultimately you will probably have to make the final decision. In your heart you'll know when the time is right. In fact, your beloved Russell will tell you himself when he gazes into your eyes one day and that look tells you that he can't go on.

Euthanasia is the kindest gift you can give to your loyal, loving companion. It literally is "going to sleep," calmly, and painlessly with dignity. Your veterinarian can explain the process to you to allay your fears and give you the support you need to get through this trying time. Many owners hold their pets in their arms as the injection is administered. It is quick, quiet, and painless, and in your heart and soul you will know that you have taken the best possible care of your loving Russell right until the end and that there is no greater love than that.

Our pets play such an important part in our lives that losing them, for many owners, is no different from losing a family member. It's normal to grieve. Some owners find it helps to talk to another person. Your veterinarian can advise you about grief counseling, should you feel the need. But probably the best way to heal your broken heart is to give it to a new, bouncing Russell, that will remind you all over again why owning and being owned by these sprightly creatures is the most magical experience imaginable!

Chapter Ten

Special Considerations

Should You Neuter Your Russell?

Unless you plan to hit the show circuit with your Russell, you should have him neutered as soon as possible. It is generally accepted that neutering male dogs is one way to prevent aggressive and other problematic behavior like territorial marking, fighting, and mounting. Because the Russell is naturally prone to aggressiveness and all its related behavioral issues, it's a good idea to neuter him. Neutering also promotes health benefits like reducing the incidence of prostate problems and completely eliminating the possibility of testicular cancer, a common malady in older, intact male dogs. Neutering is a relatively simple, low-risk procedure when performed by a competent veterinarian. There is little to no post-op care, and most dogs return home the same day. In most areas, license fees for neutered dogs are less expensive than for intact males.

If you have a female and have no intention of showing her in conformation events, she should be spayed at about six months of age. This will put her in the low-risk category for ever developing breast cancer. Additionally, because spaying entails the removal of the ovaries and uterus, there is no danger of her ever developing cancers in these organs. An unspayed female has heat periods twice a year, during which she must be confined for three to four weeks to keep her away from any unneutered males. Spaying a female will save you a lot of headaches and keep your dog healthier.

Identification

It's a heartbreaking matter when a beloved pet becomes lost. Sometimes, even the most vigilant owners are faced with this situation and must rely on the kindness of strangers to get their pet back. If your Russell is found, he can't relate his address and phone number, so it's imperative that you make sure he has proper identification. Your Russell should have a name tag with your address and phone attached to or inscribed on his collar at all times. However, don't rely on that alone to get your missing boy back. Collars can become undone or pulled off.

Tattoo

Many owners choose to have their pets tattooed as an extra safety measure. In this process, the owner's phone number or Social Security umber is permanently tattooed inside the dog's ear flap or on the inside of his thigh. It is a painless procedure. But it also has its limitations. Tattoos can fade with age or become blurred if the dog's weight changes or if he ever has a skin infection that would cause scaling. Thus, don't rely on a tattoo alone to keep your pet safe. If you do have your boy tattooed, make sure it's done on the inside of his thigh. Unbelievable as it may seem, dog nappers who sell stolen animals on the black market have been known to cut off an ear flap just to get rid of a tattoo!

Microchip

The most effective method of identification to date is the microchip. Your veterinarian injects a microscopic chip under your Russell's skin. The chip contains a serial number that contains all your pet's vital information: name, address, phone number, and veterinarian's number, and is connected to a large network where the information is registered. If your Russell becomes lost, whoever finds him can take him to any veterinarian or shelter, where a scanner will be run over the dog's back. If he has a microchip, all of his identification information will be accessed immediately, and your boy will soon be on his way back to you. Microchipping your Russell is one of the most important things you can do for him and for your own peace of mind. It is inexpensive and provides a lifetime of security for your beloved pet. After

CHECKLIST

Traveling Tips

Before you pack Jack into the car, make a simple checklist to assure that your trip will be problem free.

✔ A few days before leaving, bring your boy to the veterinarian for a quick checkup, and while you're there, get a health certificate and proof of his vaccinations. This will be useful if you need to board him during any part of your vacation. Depending on your destination, your veterinarian may want to give him some additional shots.

✔ If your travel plans include leaving the country, check beforehand if the places you are visiting require quarantine periods or more detailed documentation.

✔ If your Russell suffers from motion sickness or gets a little anxious when traveling, your veterinarian may prescribe medication to help him on the trip.

✔ Make sure your Russell has a good sturdy collar with ID tags that list your cell phone as well as home phone number. It's also a good idea to add an extra tag with your destination address and phone contact.

✔ Carry a current photograph of your dog that can be copied, to make it easier for others to recognize and return him if he gets lost.

✔ Bring along some of his comforts from home, e.g., bed or mat, favorite toys, food, treats and bowls.

✔ Bring his regular food or you'll send his gastrointestinal tract into a meltdown.

✔ Bring a gallon of water from home or used bottled water. Different local water can trigger a bout of diarrhea.

✔ Check ahead of time that the hotels or motels where you plan to stay are pet friendly. And bring a pooper scooper!

If you're traveling by car…

✔ Keep your Russell under some restraint by using either a crate or a pet barrier. You can also try a pet seat belt or restraining harness, but get your Russell used to having it on beforehand. Do not ever open a car door until you have your pet secured on his leash.

✔ Before you open the car door, even for a second, make sure the leash is on him and that you have a firm grasp. If not, you might find yourself chasing your dog through an unknown environment—or worse—traffic.

✔ Do not ever put your Russell in the back of a pickup truck. There is no harness or carrier that can save him if you must suddenly stop and he's thrown.

✔ Don't leave your dog alone in the car. The inside temperature of the car can rise to a fatal level, especially in hot weather, even if the windows are slightly open. Your dog can also be stolen from an unattended car.

✔ Make frequent stops so your Russell can relieve himself and stretch his legs.

your pet is microchipped, have the scanner run over his back each time you go to the veterinarian, just to make sure it is operating properly.

GPS Collars

GPS (Global Positioning System) collars were originally used to track wildlife. The principle is simple: The collar is equipped with a "locator" that transmits information back to a GPS receiver. When the collar is positioned on the animal, his location can be tracked on either a handheld receiver or through a central receiver. There are several variations of the GPS collar available for household pets. One of the more popular is the Zoomback Advanced GPS Dog Locator, which is available at many pet stores. It's a small water-resistant pouch containing a locator device that attaches to your dog's collar. If he strays, you can locate him via a toll-free 24/7 customer care line. The Zoomback requires a monthly service plan once the collar is activated. If your Russell is a working terrier, you might want to consider investing in a GPS collar as an extra safety measure.

Traveling with Your Russell

Your Russell is a born traveler. And why not? He was bred to hunt and explore rolling terrains. For this reason, his natural curiosity combined with his sporting nature make him an ideal travel companion. Whether you're off on a day trip, a family vacation, or hiking in the woods, your Russell will be eager to join in the fun.

Some dogs experience motion sickness when traveling by car for long periods of time. This is especially true if you haven't gotten your Russell used to car travel before the vacation trip. However, some dogs simply don't tolerate car rides as well as others.

In most cases, once you acclimate your dog to short trips in the car, he'll stop getting carsick and won't need to be medicated.

BE PREPARED! How to Avoid Motion Sickness

- Don't feed your dog before taking him on a car ride.
- Get him used to riding in the car by taking him on several short trips.
- Gradually increase the length of each ride as he becomes acclimated to the motion of the car.
- Take plenty of paper towels, newspapers, or disposable bags to shove under him if he starts to vomit.
- If he is still gets sick when you take him in the car, you can give him an over-the-counter human motion sickness drug called Bonine. Check with your veterinarian for proper dosage.

Checking for Dog-Friendly Hotels

Don't just assume that because you're registered at a hotel or motel that you can walk your Russell right into the room with you. Although many hotel and motel chains accept pets, many do not. Even those that do may require a reservation in advance. As soon as you're ready to plan your trip, first check for accommodations that are pet friendly. *Petswelcome.com* is the Internet's largest pet-travel resource with more than 25,000 listings for hotels, bed-and-breakfasts, ski resorts, camp-grounds, and beaches that are pet friendly. Just click on their "lodging listings" and check out their "travel tips" section to find out how you can take your Russell anywhere you want to visit.

CAUTION

Even under the best conditions, travel can be very stressful for your pet. Be sure to talk to your veterinarian before transporting your Russell to make sure he is sufficiently healthy to withstand the trip.

Traveling by Air with Your Russell

Many airlines will allow you to travel with a small pet in the cabin of the plane if he fits into a carry-on kennel or approved carrier that can slide under a passenger seat. Most Russells

BE PREPARED! Getting Your Russell Ready for Flight

- Whenever possible, book a direct, nonstop flight and avoid holiday or weekend travel.
- Consider schedules that minimize temperature extremes. For example, try to avoid travel during excessively hot or cold periods. Morning or evening flights are preferable during the summer.
- Check with a veterinarian to be sure that your pet is fit to travel.
- Get a health certificate from your veterinarian to comply with the rules of most airlines, as well as state and federal rules. A valid certificate must be issued no more than seven to ten days before your departure. Double-check with your airline for the exact amount of time they require before your pet's trip.
- Get an airline-approved carrier/kennel. It must be sturdy, properly ventilated, and large enough for your Russell to freely stand, turn around, and lie down. The kennel must close securely. Animal and Plant Health Inspection Service (APHIS) regulations require that the kennel have projecting rims or spacers to ensure that its ventilation slats cannot be blocked by adjoining kennels or cargo. Appropriate kennels are available at pet stores and from most airlines. Remember to check with your airline, because airline policies can vary.
- Clearly display your name and address on the outside of the kennel, using arrows to indicate the top and bottom.
- Display labels on top and on at least one side with the words LIVE ANIMAL printed in large letters.
- Secure empty food and water dishes inside the kennel that are accessible from the outside.
- If your pet will require food, for example, during stopovers, attach a bag of food to the outside of the kennel with feeding instructions.
- Place absorbent material or bedding, such as newspaper, inside the kennel.

meet this size requirement. If the airline does not allow you to bring your Russell into the cabin, he will have to travel in a special hold in the cargo area, which is fully pressurized for his comfort and safety. There are some airlines, however, that do not allow pets under any circumstances. Make sure you check with your airline before making a reservation and be sure to mention that you want to bring your pet. Most airline websites have this information readily available. If not, call the airline directly and ask about their pet policy. If your Russell is a registered service animal, different rules apply. Check with your airline.

Should You Sedate Your Russell Before Air Travel?

Most veterinarians advise against sedation because the effects of tranquilizers on animals at high altitudes can be unpredictable. The decision to prescribe a tranquilizer for your pet should be made by you and your veterinarian.

Kenneling Your Russell

Often when the family goes on vacation, they prefer to send their pet on "vacation," too. Whether or not your pet will be happy with this decision largely depends on the place you choose to board him. There are many excellent boarding kennels that can take care of your Russell's needs while you are gone. Many veterinarians also provide boarding services. If you decide to send your boy to a kennel, do your homework. Find a place where he will have lots of care, stimulation, and fun. Kennels range from bare-bones spare to the very plush with private suites rivaling the best hotels. High-end kennels offer pets every comfort of home, including such things as piped-in music, television, plush bedding, and personalized playtime. Keep in mind that the more amenities, the pricier the kennel. All your boy really needs is a safe, comfortable place with a professional staff dedicated to making his time away from home a happy and healthy one.

Before selecting a kennel, ask your veterinarian and other dog friends for a recommendation. Then, visit the kennel yourself and make sure it meets your standards.

When selecting a boarding kennel for your Russell, don't be afraid to ask lots of questions and ask for references. If the kennel manager seems the

CHECKLIST

What to Look for in a Boarding Kennel

✔ Is it generally clean and free of bad odors?

✔ Does it provide clean, well-ventilated, and well-sized indoor/outdoor runs?

✔ Is there sufficient staff to take care of the number of animals boarded?

✔ Is the staff knowledgeable enough to recognize and handle an emergency, should it arise?

✔ Will your dog be walked in a secure area several times a day and have daily playtime?

✔ Will your dog be fed his regular food and treats?

✔ If your Russell has special needs, such as medication or exercise, are they able and willing to handle it?

✔ Will they provide you with scheduled updates of your pet's condition if you ask?

✔ Is there a veterinarian on call 24 hours a day?

✔ Is there 24-hour supervision by a licensed attendant?

You may also have additional requests or services you want performed. Be sure to get a price quote in advance for all that you require for your Russell's stay at the kennel. While his "vacation" may not be cheap, it's a small price to pay to ensure that your boy is being well cared for while you're away.

least bit reluctant, leave immediately and find another kennel. It's also a good idea to check out the occupants of the kennel when you visit. Do the other dogs appear clean, happy, and well cared for? Is someone walking them and playing with them or are they being left alone in cages with no stimulation? Are the attendants wearing clean clothes and smocks? All of these things signal how the kennel is being run and should influence your decision to leave your Russell there for any length of time.

Before dropping your Russell off at a kennel, he will need to have a health certificate with proof of his shots from your veterinarian. Also be sure to leave your veterinarian's phone number in case a medical condition should arise.

Pet-Sitting Services

Some owners are reluctant to remove their pet from the safety and comfort of his home while they are away on vacation and prefer to use a pet-sitting service or a pet sitter. This is becoming a more popular practice because it reduces the amount of stress your pet will experience while you are gone. If you engage a pet-sitting service, make sure it is licensed and bonded and ask for references. Reputable pet sitting services will provide you with a contract detailing their services and rates. You can also add specific requests above and beyond what they offer. If you hire a pet sitter, make sure he or she comes

highly recommended. Do not leave your dog with a boy or girl who lives in the neighborhood and has offered to take care of him while you are away. It's best to get a recommendation from your veterinarian or simply hire a mature, experienced person you know who also knows and loves your dog.

Relocating Your Russell

If you take a new job or are transferred to another state or even another country, you'll need to make moving arrangements for your Russell. The very idea can be daunting. But thanks to an ever-expanding global moving and travel support service system, relocating your pet has never been easier or lower stress than it is today. If you and your family are relocating a great distance, it may be easier to make separate moving arrangements for your Russell to assure that he will be transported safely and under professional supervision. The job of a pet relocation service is to see to your pet's comfort and supervise his transport every step of the way, including delivery to his new address, and transfers and pickup at airports. Every aspect of the process is personalized and organized down to the smallest detail. Although these services are not inexpensive (reputable services like *PetRelocation.com* start at $800–$1,000 within the United States), they do take the stress out of having to relocate your pet. Before you hire a pet transport service, be sure to check their credentials.

Helpful Hints

You can also elect to transport your Russell via a licensed pet travel service that handles pick-up and delivery of your pet.

Resources

Kennel and Breed Clubs
American Kennel Club (AKC)
5580 Centerview Drive
Raleigh, NC 27606-3390
(919) 233-9767
E-mail: info@akc.org
www.akc.org

American Working Terrier
    Association (AWTA)
www.dirt-dog.com/awta

Canadian Kennel Club (CKC)
89 Skyway Avenue, Suite 100
Etobicoke
Ontario, Canada M9W 6R4
(416) 675-5511
www.ckc.ca

Earthdog Clubs
www.canineworld/earthdogclubs

The Jack Russell Terrier Club
    of America (JRTCA)
www.jrtca.com

WPAEarthdog
Champion, PA
www.wpaearthdog.org

North American Dog Agility
    Council
HCR 2, Box 277
St. Maries, ID 83861
(208) 689-3803

Parson Russell Terrier Association
    of America (PRTAA)
www.prtaa.org

States Kennel Club
1007 W. Pine Street
Hattiesburg, MS 39401
(601) 583-8345

United Kennel Club (UKC)
100 E.Kilgore Road
Kalamazoo, MI 49001-5598
(616) 343-9020

United States Dog Agility
    Association
P.O. Box 850955
Richardson, TX 75085-8955
(972) 231-9700
E-mail: info@usdaa.com
www.usdaa.com

Health-Related Associations and Foundations
American College of Veterinary
    Internal Medicine
Cardiology
7175 W. Jefferson Avenue, Suite 2125
Lakewood, CO 80235-2320
Phone: (800) 245-9081
Fax: (303) 980-7136

American Holistic Veterinary
    Medical Association (AHVMA)
2218 Old Emmorton Road
Bel Air, MD 21015
(410) 569-0795
www.ahvma.org

American Kennel Club Canine
   Health Foundation
251 W. Garfield Road, Suite 160
Aurora, OH 44202-8856
Phone: (330) 995-0807
Fax: (330) 995-0806
E-mail: AKCCHF@aol.com
www.akcchf.org

American Kennel Club
DNA Operations & Educational
   Services
Phone: (919) 854-0108
Fax: (919) 854-0102
E-mail: dna@akc.org

American Society for the
   Prevention of Cruelty
   to Animals (ASPCA)
424 E. 92nd Street
New York, NY 10128-6801
(212) 876-7700
www.aspca.org

American Veterinary Medical
   Association (AVMA)
930 North Meacham Road
Schaumberg, IL 60173
www.avma.org

Canine Eye Registration Foundation
   VMDB/CERF
248 Lynn Hall
Purdue University
West Lafayette, IN 47906
(765) 494-8179
www.vmdb.org/cerf.html

College of Veterinary Medicine
   Michigan State University
Attention: Diagnostic Lab (thyroid)
P.O. Box 30076
Lansing, MI 48909-7576
(517) 353-0621

Delta Society
289 Perimeter Road E.
Renton, WA 98055
(800) 869-6898
www.deltasociety@cis.compuserve.com

The Humane Society of the
   United States (HSUS)
2100 L Street, NW
Washington, DC 20037
(202) 452-1100
www.hsus.org

Institute for Genetic Disease Control
   in Animals
P.O. Box 222
Davis, CA 95617
(916) 756-6773
www.gdcinstitute.org/maininfo.htm

National Animal Poison Control
   Center
1717 S. Philo Road, Suite 36
Urbana, IL 61802
(800) 4ANI-HELP
(900) 680-0000

Orthopedic Foundation for
   Animals (OFA)
2300 Nifong Boulevard
Columbia, MO 65201-3856
(573) 875-5073
www.offa.org

PennHip
c/o Synbiotics Corporation
(800) 228-4305

School of Veterinary Medicine—
   Deafness
Communication Sciences &
   Disorders
Louisiana State University
Baton Rouge, LA 70803
www.1su.edu/deafness/deaf.htm

Therapy Dogs International
88 Bartley Road
Flanders, NJ 07836
(973) 252-9800
E-mail: tdi@gti.net
www.tdi-dog.org

VetGen Canine Genetic Services—
  DNA
3728 Plaza Drive, Suite 1
Ann Arbor, MI 48108
(800) 483-8436 or (734) 669-8440
www.vetgen.com

Lost Pet Registries

American Kennel Club (AKC)
  AKC Companion Recovery
5580 Centerview Drive, Suite 250
Raleigh, NC 27606-3394
(800) 252-7894
E-mail: found@akc.org
www.akc.org/car.htm

AVID PETtrac
3179 Hamner Avenue
Norco, CA 92860-9972
(800) 336-AVID
E-mail: PETtrac@AvidID.com
www.avidmicrochip.com

Home Again Microchip Service
(800) LONELY-ONE
http://public.homeagain.com

National Dog Registry (NDR)
P.O. Box 118
Woodstock, NY 12498-0116
(800) 637-3647

Petfinders
368 High Street
Athol, NY 12810
(800) 223-4747

Training

Association of Pet Dog Trainers
  (APDT)
150 Executive Center Drive
Box 35
Greenville, SC 29615
(800) PET-DOGS
www.apdt.com

National Association of Dog
  Obedience Instructors (NADOI)
PMB 369
729 Grapevine Highway
Hurst, TX 76054-2085
www.nadoi.org

Pet Sitters

National Association of Professional
  Pet Sitters
15000 Commerce Parkway, Suite C
Mt. Laurel, NJ 08054
(856) 439-0324
www.petsitters.org

Pet Sitters International
201 East King Street
King, NC 27021-9161
(336) 983-9222
www.petsit.com

Periodicals

The American Kennel Club Gazette
51 Madison Avenue
New York, NY 10010

Dog Fancy
P.O. Box 53264
Boulder, CO 80323-3264
(303) 786-7306 / 666-8504
www.dogfancy.com

Dog World
29 North Wacker Drive
Chicago, IL 60606
(312) 726-2802

Down to Earth
www.dirtdog.com

Parson's Nook
The Parson Russell Terrier
  Association of America
www.prtaa.org

Books

Boneham, Sheila, Ph.D. *The Parson &*
  Jack Russell Terriers. Neptune City,
  NJ: TFH Publications, 2006.
Brown, Catherine Romaine. *The Jack*
  Russell Terrier. New York: Howell
  Book House, 1999.
The Complete Dog Book; Official
  Publication of the American Kennel
  Club. New York: Howell Book
  House, 1992.
Jackson, Jean and Frank. *Parson*
  Jack Russell Terriers: An Owner's
  Companion. New York: Random
  House, 1990.
Jack Russell Terriers Today.
  Gloucestershire, GB: Ringpress
  Books Ltd., 1995.
Kosloff, George. *Guide to Owning a*
  Jack Russell Terrier. Neptune City,
  NJ: TFH Publications, 1999.
Leighton, Robert. *Dogs and All About*
  Them. Whitefish, MT: Kessinger
  Publishing, Reprinted, 2004.
Plummer, D. Brian. *The Complete Jack*
  Russell Terrier. New York: Howell
  Book House, 1980.

Websites of Interest

www.dogplay.com

www.infodog.com

www.petswelcome.com

www.PetRelocation.com

Index

THE TEAM BEHIND THE *TRAIN YOUR DOG* DVD

Host **Nicole Wilde** is a certified Pet Dog Trainer and internationally recognized author and lecturer. Her books include *So You Want to be a Dog Trainer* and *Help for Your Fearful Dog* (Phantom Publishing). In addition to working with dogs, Nicole has been working with wolves and wolf hybrids for over fifteen years and is considered an expert in the field.

Host **Laura Bourhenne** is a Professional Member of the Association of Pet Dog Trainers, and holds a degree in Exotic Animal Training. She has trained many species of animals including several species of primates, birds of prey, and many more. Laura is striving to enrich the lives of pets by training and educating the people they live with.

Director **Leo Zahn** is an award winning director/cinematographer/editor of television commercials, movies, and documentaries. He has directed and edited more than a dozen instructional DVDs through the Picture Company, a subsidiary of Picture Palace, Inc., based in Los Angeles.